TACOS

AND MORE

Publications International, Ltd.

Pictured on the front cover *(clockwise from top left):* Mexican-Style Corn on the Cob *(page 134)*, Strawberry Margarita *(page 160)*, Salsa *(page 20)*, Guacamole *(page 20)* and Simple Shredded Pork Tacos *(page 70)*.

Pictured on the back cover *(clockwise from top left):* Island Fish Tacos *(page 36)*, Turkey and Winter Squash Tacos *(page 110)*, Tacos with Carnitas *(page 66)*, White Spinach Queso *(page 6)* and Corn Tortilla Chips *(page 16)*.

Let's get social!

@Publications_International

@PublicationsInternational

www.pilbooks.com

CONTENTS

APPETIZERS

WHITE SPINACH QUESO

1 tablespoon olive oil

1 clove garlic, minced

1 tablespoon all-purpose flour

1 can (12 ounces) evaporated milk

½ teaspoon salt

2 cups (8 ounces) shredded Monterey Jack cheese, divided

1 package (10 ounces) frozen chopped spinach, thawed and squeezed dry

Optional toppings: pico de gallo, guacamole, chopped fresh cilantro and queso fresco

Tortilla chips

1 Preheat broiler.

2 Heat oil in medium saucepan over medium-low heat. Add garlic; cook and stir 1 minute without browning. Add flour; whisk until smooth. Add evaporated milk in thin, steady stream, whisking constantly. Stir in salt. Cook 4 minutes or until slightly thickened, whisking frequently. Add 1½ cups Monterey Jack cheese; whisk until smooth. Stir in spinach. Pour into medium cast iron skillet; sprinkle with remaining ½ cup Monterey Jack cheese.

3 Broil 1 minute or until cheese is melted and browned in spots. Top as desired. Serve immediately with tortilla chips.

VEGGIE QUESADILLA APPETIZERS

2 cups Zesty Pico de Gallo (recipe follows)

10 (8-inch) flour tortillas

1 cup finely chopped broccoli

1 cup thinly sliced small mushrooms

¾ cup shredded carrots

¼ cup chopped green onions

1¼ cups (5 ounces) shredded sharp Cheddar cheese

1 Prepare Zesty Pico de Gallo.

2 Brush both sides of tortillas lightly with water. Heat small nonstick skillet over medium heat. Heat tortillas, one at a time, 30 seconds on each side. Divide vegetables among 5 tortillas; sprinkle evenly with cheese. Top with remaining 5 tortillas.

3 Cook quesadillas, one at a time, in large nonstick skillet or on griddle over medium heat 2 minutes on each side or until surface is crisp and cheese is melted.

4 Cut each quesadilla into 4 wedges. Serve with Zesty Pico de Gallo.

ZESTY PICO DE GALLO

2 cups chopped seeded tomatoes

1 cup chopped green onions

1 can (about 8 ounces) tomato sauce

½ cup minced fresh cilantro

1 to 2 tablespoons minced jalapeño peppers

1 tablespoon fresh lime juice

Combine tomatoes, green onions, tomato sauce, cilantro, jalapeños and lime juice in medium bowl; stir to blend. Cover and refrigerate at least 1 hour.

GUACAMOLE BITES

2 tablespoons vegetable oil
1¼ teaspoons salt, divided
½ teaspoon garlic powder
12 (6-inch) corn tortillas
2 small ripe avocados
2 tablespoons finely chopped onion
1 tablespoon chopped fresh cilantro
2 teaspoons lime juice
1 teaspoon finely chopped jalapeño pepper *or* ¼ teaspoon hot pepper sauce

1 Preheat oven to 375°F. Whisk oil, ¾ teaspoon salt and garlic powder in small bowl until well blended.

2 Use 3-inch biscuit cutter to cut out two circles from each tortilla to create 24 circles total. Wrap stack of tortilla circles loosely in waxed paper; microwave on HIGH 10 to 15 seconds or just until softened. Brush one side of each tortilla very lightly with oil mixture; press into 24 mini (1¾-inch) muffin cups, oiled side up. (Do not spray muffin cups with nonstick cooking spray.)

3 Bake 8 minutes or until crisp. Remove to wire racks to cool.

4 Meanwhile, prepare guacamole. Cut avocados into halves; remove pits. Scoop pulp into large bowl; mash roughly, leaving avocado slightly chunky. Stir in onion, cilantro, lime juice, remaining ½ teaspoon salt and jalapeño; mix well.

5 Fill each tortilla cup with 2 to 3 teaspoons guacamole.

CHICKEN FAJITA NACHOS

2 tablespoons vegetable oil, divided

2 red bell peppers, cut into thin strips

1 large onion, cut in half and thinly sliced

2 tablespoons fajita seasoning mix (from 1¼-ounce package), divided

2 tablespoons water, divided

1 large boneless skinless chicken breast (about 12 ounces), cut into 2×1-inch strips

4 cups tortilla chips (about 30 chips)

½ cup (2 ounces) shredded Cheddar cheese

½ cup (2 ounces) shredded Monterey Jack cheese

1 jalapeño pepper, seeded and thinly sliced

1 cup shredded lettuce

½ cup salsa

Sour cream and guacamole (optional)

1 Heat 1 tablespoon oil in large skillet over medium-high heat. Add bell peppers and onion; cook 5 minutes or until tender and browned in spots, stirring frequently. Remove to large bowl; stir in 1 tablespoon fajita seasoning mix and 1 tablespoon water.

2 Heat remaining 1 tablespoon oil in same skillet over medium-high heat. Add chicken; cook 7 to 10 minutes or until cooked through, stirring occasionally. Add remaining 1 tablespoon fajita seasoning mix and 1 tablespoon water; cook and stir 3 to 5 minutes or until chicken is coated.

3 Preheat broiler. Spread chips in 11×7-inch baking dish or pan; top with vegetables, chicken, Cheddar and Monterey Jack cheeses and jalapeño pepper.

4 Broil 2 to 4 minutes or until cheeses are melted. Top with lettuce and salsa; serve with sour cream and guacamole, if desired.

CHICKEN ENCHILADA SOUP

2 tablespoons vegetable oil, divided

1½ pounds boneless skinless chicken breasts, cut into ½-inch pieces

½ cup chopped onion

2 cloves garlic, minced

2 cans (about 14 ounces each) chicken broth

3 cups water, divided

1 cup masa harina

1 package (16 ounces) pasteurized process cheese product, cubed

1 can (10 ounces) mild red enchilada sauce

1 teaspoon chili powder

½ teaspoon salt

½ teaspoon ground cumin

1 large tomato, seeded and chopped

Crispy tortilla strips*

If tortilla strips are not available, crumble tortilla chips into 1-inch pieces.

1 Heat 1 tablespoon oil in large saucepan or Dutch oven over medium-high heat. Add chicken; cook and stir 10 minutes or until no longer pink. Transfer to medium bowl with slotted spoon; drain excess liquid from saucepan.

2 Heat remaining 1 tablespoon oil in same saucepan over medium-high heat. Add onion and garlic; cook and stir 3 minutes or until softened. Stir in broth.

3 Whisk 2 cups water into masa harina in large bowl until smooth. Whisk mixture into broth in saucepan. Stir in remaining 1 cup water, cheese product, enchilada sauce, chili powder, salt and cumin; bring to a boil over high heat. Add chicken. Reduce heat to medium-low; simmer 30 minutes, stirring frequently. Ladle soup into bowls; top with tomato and tortilla strips.

CORN TORTILLA CHIPS

12 (6-inch) corn tortillas,
    preferably day-old
Vegetable oil
½ to 1 teaspoon salt

1 If tortillas are fresh, let stand, uncovered, in single layer on wire rack 1 to 2 hours to dry slightly.

2 Stack 6 tortillas; cutting through stack, cut tortillas into 6 or 8 equal wedges. Repeat with remaining tortillas.

3 Heat ½ inch oil in deep, heavy, large skillet over medium-high heat to 375°F; adjust heat to maintain temperature.

4 Fry tortilla wedges in a single layer 1 minute or until crisp, turning occasionally. Remove with slotted spoon; drain on paper towels. Repeat until all chips have been fried. Sprinkle chips with salt.

NOTE

Tortilla chips are served with salsa as a snack, used as the base for nachos and used as scoops for guacamole, other dips or refried beans. They are best eaten fresh, but can be stored, tightly covered, in cool place 2 or 3 days. Reheat in 350°F oven a few minutes before serving.

BLACK BEAN SOUP

2 tablespoons vegetable oil

1 cup diced onion

1 stalk celery, diced

2 carrots, diced

½ small green bell pepper, diced

4 cloves garlic, minced

4 cans (about 15 ounces each) black beans, rinsed and drained, divided

4 cups (32 ounces) chicken or vegetable broth, divided

2 tablespoons cider vinegar

2 teaspoons chili powder

½ teaspoon salt

½ teaspoon ground red pepper

½ teaspoon ground cumin

¼ teaspoon liquid smoke

Optional toppings: sour cream, chopped green onions and/or shredded Cheddar cheese

1 Heat oil in large saucepan or Dutch oven over medium-low heat. Add onion, celery, carrots, bell pepper and garlic; cook 10 minutes, stirring occasionally.

2 Combine half of beans and 1 cup broth in food processor or blender; process until smooth. Add to vegetables in saucepan.

3 Stir in remaining beans, remaining 3 cups broth, vinegar, chili powder, salt, red pepper, cumin and liquid smoke; bring to a boil over high heat. Reduce heat to medium-low. Cook 1 hour or until vegetables are tender and soup is thickened. Garnish as desired.

GUACAMOLE

MAKES 2 CUPS ▶

2 large ripe avocados
2 teaspoons fresh lime juice
¼ cup finely chopped red onion
2 tablespoons chopped fresh
cilantro
½ jalapeño pepper, finely
chopped
½ teaspoon salt

1 Cut avocados in half lengthwise around pits. Remove pits. Scoop avocados into large bowl; sprinkle with lime juice and toss to coat. Mash to desired consistency with fork or potato masher.

2 Add onion, cilantro, jalapeño and salt; stir gently until well blended. Add additional salt, if desired.

SALSA

MAKES 4½ CUPS

1 can (28 ounces) whole Italian
plum tomatoes, undrained
2 fresh plum tomatoes, seeded
and coarsely chopped
¼ cup chopped fresh cilantro
¼ cup chopped green onions
2 tablespoons canned diced
mild green chiles
1 tablespoon canned diced
jalapeño peppers
1 tablespoon white vinegar
1 clove garlic, minced
1 teaspoon onion powder
1 teaspoon sugar
1 teaspoon ground cumin
½ teaspoon garlic powder
¼ teaspoon salt

Combine tomatoes with juice, fresh tomatoes, cilantro, green onions, green chiles, jalapeño peppers, vinegar, garlic, onion powder, sugar, cumin, garlic powder and salt in food processor or blender; process until finely chopped.

GAZPACHO

6 large, very ripe tomatoes
(about 3 pounds), divided

1½ cups tomato juice

1 clove garlic

2 tablespoons fresh lime juice

2 tablespoons olive oil

1 tablespoon white wine
vinegar

1 teaspoon sugar

½ to 1 teaspoon salt

½ teaspoon dried oregano

6 green onions, sliced

¼ cup finely chopped celery

¼ cup finely chopped seeded
cucumber

1 or 2 fresh jalapeño peppers,
seeded and minced

Garlic Croutons (recipe
follows) or packaged
croutons (optional)

1 cup diced avocado

1 red or green bell pepper,
chopped

2 tablespoons chopped fresh
cilantro

Lime wedges and sour cream
(optional)

1 Seed and finely chop 1 tomato; set aside.

2 Coarsely chop remaining 5 tomatoes; process half of tomatoes, ¾ cup tomato juice and garlic in blender until smooth. Press through sieve into large bowl; discard seeds. Repeat with remaining coarsely chopped tomatoes and ¾ cup tomato juice.

3 Whisk lime juice, oil, vinegar, sugar, salt and oregano into tomato mixture. Stir in finely chopped tomato, onions, celery, cucumber and jalapeño pepper. Cover; refrigerate at least 4 hours or up to 24 hours to develop flavors.

4 Prepare Garlic Croutons, if desired. Stir soup; ladle into chilled bowls. Top with croutons, avocado, bell pepper and cilantro. Serve with lime wedges and sour cream, if desired.

GARLIC CROUTONS

5 slices firm white bread
2 tablespoons olive oil
1 clove garlic, minced
¼ teaspoon paprika

1 Preheat oven to 300°F. Trim crusts from bread; cut into ½-inch cubes.

2 Heat oil in skillet over medium heat. Stir in garlic and paprika. Add bread; cook and stir 1 minute just until bread is evenly coated with oil.

3 Spread bread on baking sheet. Bake 20 to 25 minutes until crisp and golden. Cool.

NACHOS

8 (6-inch) corn tortillas

1 cup chopped onion

1 tablespoon chili powder

2 teaspoons dried oregano

1 can (about 15 ounces) pinto beans or black beans, rinsed and drained

1¼ cups (5 ounces) shredded Monterey Jack cheese

¾ cup frozen corn, thawed and drained

1 jar (2 ounces) pimientos, drained

3 tablespoons sliced black olives

2 to 3 tablespoons pickled jalapeño pepper slices, drained

1 Preheat oven to 375°F. Sprinkle 1 tortilla with water to dampen; shake off excess water. Repeat with remaining tortillas. Cut each tortilla into 6 wedges. Arrange wedges in single layer on baking sheet or in two 9-inch pie plates. Bake 4 minutes. Rotate sheet. Bake another 2 to 4 minutes or until chips are firm; do not let brown. Remove chips to plate to cool. Set aside.

2 Spray medium saucepan with nonstick cooking spray; heat over medium-high heat. Add onion; cook and stir 6 to 8 minutes or until onion is tender. Add chili powder and oregano; cook and stir 1 minute. Remove from heat. Add beans and 2 tablespoons water; mash with fork or potato masher until blended but still chunky. Cover; cook over medium heat 6 to 8 minutes or until bubbly, stirring occasionally. Stir in additional water if beans become dry.

3 Sprinkle cheese evenly over chips. Spoon beans over chips. Combine corn and pimientos in small bowl; spoon over beans. Bake 8 minutes or until cheese is melted. Sprinkle with olives and jalapeños.

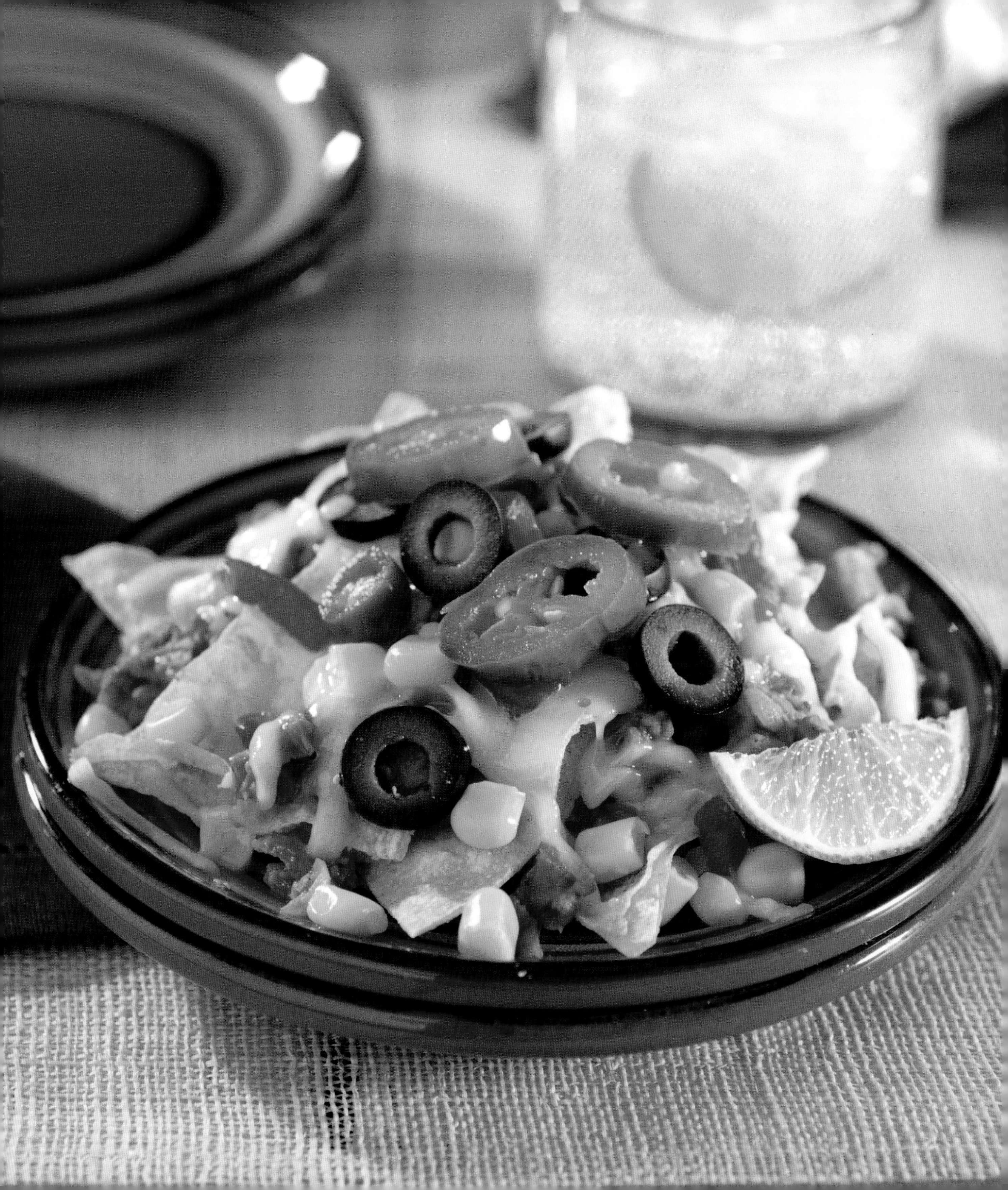

CORN AND JALAPEÑO CHOWDER

MAKES 4 SERVINGS ▶

4 cups frozen whole-kernel corn, thawed and divided

2 cups chicken broth, divided

2 jalapeño peppers, seeded and finely chopped

¼ teaspoon onion salt

1½ teaspoons whole cumin seeds, crushed

1 cup half-and-half

¼ cup (1 ounce) shredded Cheddar cheese

¼ cup thinly sliced roasted red pepper

1 Combine 2 cups corn and 1 cup broth in food processor. Cover; process until nearly smooth.

2 Stir together blended corn mixture, remaining corn, remaining broth, jalapeño peppers, onion salt and cumin seeds in large saucepan. Bring to a boil. Reduce heat. Cover; simmer 5 minutes.

3 Stir in half-and-half; cook until heated through. Sprinkle each serving evenly with cheese and red pepper.

LAYERED MEXICAN DIP

MAKES 10 SERVINGS

1 package (8 ounces) cream cheese, softened

1 tablespoon plus 1 teaspoon taco seasoning mix

1 cup canned black beans

1 cup salsa

1 cup shredded lettuce

1 cup (4 ounces) shredded Cheddar cheese

½ cup chopped green onions

2 tablespoons sliced pitted black olives

Tortilla chips

1 Combine cream cheese and taco seasoning mix in small bowl. Spread on bottom of 9-inch pie plate.

2 Layer black beans, salsa, lettuce, cheese, green onions and olives over cream cheese mixture. Refrigerate until ready to serve. Serve with tortilla chips.

CHORIZO AND QUESO FUNDIDO

2 cured chorizo sausages*
(about 3½ ounces total),
finely chopped

1 package (8 ounces) cream
cheese, cubed

8 ounces Monterey Jack
cheese, cubed

8 ounces pasteurized process
cheese product, cubed

8 ounces Cheddar cheese,
cubed

1 tablespoon Worcestershire
sauce

Tortilla chips

*There are two styles of chorizo
widely available in most major
supermarkets. Mexican-style,
or uncured, chorizo is typically
sold in ½- or 1-pound refrigerated
packages. Spanish-style, or cured,
chorizo is sold in links of varying
sizes held together by their
casings.*

SLOW COOKER DIRECTIONS

Combine chorizo, cream cheese, Monterey Jack cheese, cheese product, Cheddar cheese and Worcestershire sauce in 3½- to 4-quart slow cooker. Cover; cook on HIGH 1 to 1½ hours or until cheeses are softened. Whisk to blend. *Turn slow cooker to LOW or WARM.* Serve with tortilla chips.

TIP

In Spanish, queso fundido means "melted cheese," which precisely describes this dish. For a more authentic taste, replace some of the cheeses with Mexican cheeses such as queso fresco, chihuahua or cotija.

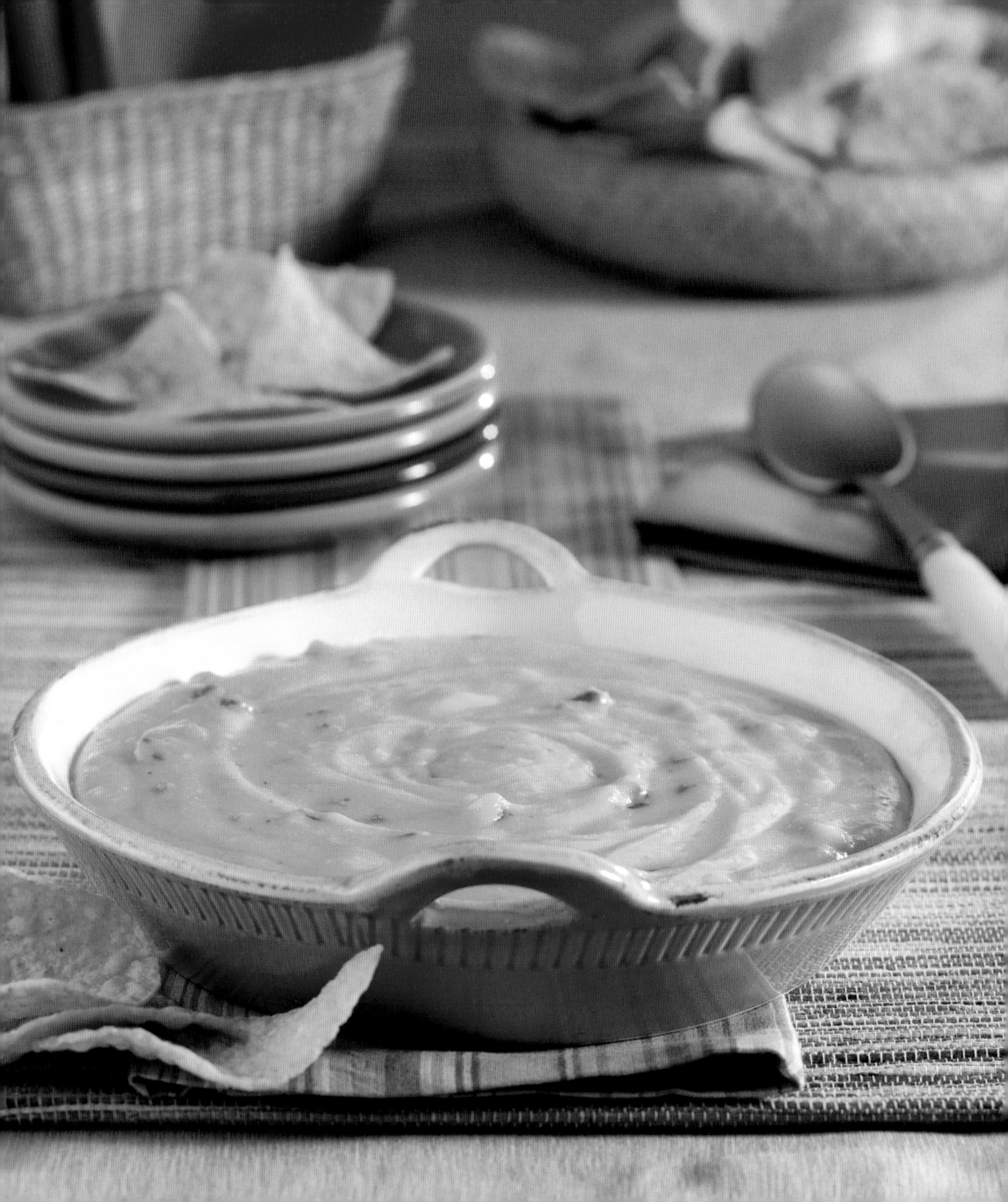

BLACK BEAN SALSA DIP
WITH VEGETABLES

1 can (about 11 ounces) condensed black bean soup
½ cup Pace® Chunky Salsa
Shredded Cheddar cheese
Sliced pitted ripe olives
Sliced green onions
Sour cream
Fresh vegetables **or** tortilla chips

1 Stir the soup and salsa in a small bowl. Cover the bowl and refrigerate for 2 hours.

2 Top the soup mixture with the cheese, olives, onions and sour cream. Serve with the fresh vegetables for dipping.

CREAMY SALSA DIP

1 cup HELLMANN'S® or BEST FOODS® Real Mayonnaise
1 cup chunky salsa, drained if desired

Combine HELLMANN'S® or BEST FOODS® Real Mayonnaise with salsa in medium bowl. Serve with baby carrots, sliced cucumbers, bell peppers, sugar snap peas and/or tortilla chips.

LIME-BEER CHICKEN NACHOS

1 cup beer

4 tablespoons fresh lime juice, divided

3 cloves garlic, minced

1 teaspoon ground cumin

¾ pound boneless skinless chicken thighs

1 pint grape tomatoes, halved

1 avocado, cut into ½-inch cubes

¼ cup finely chopped red onion

1 tablespoon chopped fresh cilantro

½ teaspoon salt, divided

1 tablespoon olive oil

¼ teaspoon black pepper

6 ounces restaurant-style tortilla chips

1 cup pasteurized process cheese product

1 Combine beer, 3 tablespoons lime juice, garlic and cumin in medium bowl; stir to blend. Add chicken; stir to coat. Cover; refrigerate 1 hour or up to 4 hours.

2 Meanwhile, combine tomatoes, avocado, onion, cilantro, remaining 1 tablespoon lime juice and ¼ teaspoon salt in large bowl; reserve.

3 Preheat oven to 400°F.

4 Lightly oil grill pan. Heat over medium-high heat. Remove chicken from beer marinade and sprinkle with remaining ¼ teaspoon salt and pepper. Add to grill pan; cook, turning once, 6 to 7 minutes per side or until thermometer inserted into thickest part of chicken registers 170°F. Remove to large cutting board; slice into thin strips.

5 Place tortilla chips on baking sheet; bake 4 to 5 minutes until heated through. Meanwhile, microwave cheese spread according to package directions until heated through.

6 Arrange half of tortilla chips on serving platter. Top with half of avocado mixture and half of chicken strips. Drizzle with half of melted cheese spread. Top with remaining chips, avocado mixture, chicken and cheese product. Serve immediately.

SEAFOOD TACOS

ISLAND FISH TACOS

COLESLAW

- 1 medium jicama (about 12 ounces), peeled and shredded
- 2 cups packaged coleslaw mix
- 3 tablespoons finely chopped fresh cilantro
- ¼ cup lime juice
- ¼ cup vegetable oil
- 3 tablespoons white vinegar
- 2 tablespoons mayonnaise
- 1 tablespoon honey
- 1 teaspoon salt

SALSA

- 2 medium fresh tomatoes, diced (about 2 cups)
- ½ cup finely chopped red onion
- ¼ cup finely chopped fresh cilantro
- 2 tablespoons lime juice
- 2 tablespoons minced jalapeño pepper
- 1 teaspoon salt

TACOS

- 1 to 1¼ pounds white fish such as tilapia or mahi mahi, cut into 3×1½-inch pieces
- Salt and black pepper
- 2 tablespoons vegetable oil
- 12 (6-inch) taco-size tortillas, heated
- Prepared guacamole (optional)

1 For coleslaw, combine jicama, coleslaw mix and 3 tablespoons cilantro in medium bowl. Whisk ¼ cup lime juice, ¼ cup oil, vinegar, mayonnaise, honey and 1 teaspoon salt in small bowl until well blended. Pour over vegetable mixture; stir to coat. Let stand at least 15 minutes for flavors to blend.

2 For salsa, place tomatoes in fine-mesh strainer; set in bowl or sink to drain 15 minutes. Transfer to another medium bowl. Stir in onion, ¼ cup cilantro, 2 tablespoons lime juice, jalapeño pepper and 1 teaspoon salt; mix well.

3 For tacos, season both sides of fish with salt and black pepper. Heat 1 tablespoon oil in large nonstick skillet over medium-high heat. Add half of fish; cook 2 minutes per side or until fish is opaque and begins to flake when tested with fork. Repeat with remaining oil and fish.

4 Serve fish in tortillas with coleslaw and salsa. Serve with guacamole, if desired.

FISH TACOS
WITH CILANTRO CREAM SAUCE

½ cup sour cream

¼ cup chopped fresh cilantro

1¼ teaspoons ground cumin, divided

1 pound skinless tilapia, mahi mahi or other firm white fish fillets

1 teaspoon garlic salt

1 teaspoon chipotle hot pepper sauce, divided

2 teaspoons canola or vegetable oil

1 red bell pepper, cut into strips

1 green bell pepper, cut into strips

8 (6-inch) corn tortillas, warmed

4 limes, cut into wedges

1 Combine sour cream, cilantro and ¼ teaspoon cumin in small bowl; mix well. Refrigerate until ready to serve.

2 Cut fish into 1-inch pieces; place in medium bowl. Add remaining 1 teaspoon cumin, garlic salt and ½ teaspoon hot pepper sauce; toss gently to coat.

3 Heat oil in large nonstick skillet over medium heat. Add fish; cook 3 to 4 minutes or until center is opaque, turning once. Remove to plate. Add bell peppers to skillet; cook 6 to 8 minutes or until tender, stirring occasionally.

4 Return fish to skillet with remaining ½ teaspoon hot pepper sauce; cook and stir just until heated through. Serve in tortillas with sauce and lime wedges.

BEER AND CHIPOTLE FISH TACOS

1½ pounds cod, grouper or other white fish fillets, cut into thin strips

1 bottle (12 ounces) light-colored beer, such as pale ale

½ cup yellow cornmeal

1 teaspoon chipotle chili powder

½ teaspoon salt

2 tablespoons olive oil

8 (6-inch) flour tortillas, warmed

1½ cups shredded cabbage

Chopped fresh tomatoes

Lime wedges (optional)

1 Place fish in shallow dish. Pour beer over fish; marinate 15 to 30 minutes.

2 Combine cornmeal, chili powder and salt in separate shallow dish. Dredge fish in cornmeal mixture; turn to coat.

3 Heat oil in large skillet over medium-high heat. Add fish; cook 3 to 4 minutes on each side or until fish begins to flake when tested with fork.

4 Place fish in tortillas. Top with cabbage and tomatoes. Garnish with lime wedges.

CITRUS CRAB TACOS WITH APRICOT COCKTAIL SAUCE

MAKES 12 TACOS

1 can lump crabmeat (cooked)
1 lemon, juiced
1 lime, juiced
1 tablespoon chopped cilantro
2 plum tomatoes, finely chopped
1 tablespoon seafood seasoning
   Salt and black pepper, to taste
1 cup **HEINZ® Original Cocktail Sauce**
3 tablespoons apricot preserves
12 small flour tortillas
1 bunch baby arugula
1 pint alfalfa sprouts

1 In a medium mixing bowl, add crabmeat, lemon and lime juice, chopped cilantro, tomatoes and seafood seasoning, and mix well. Season with salt and pepper to taste and place in fridge until ready to serve.

2 In a food processor, add Cocktail Sauce and apricot preserves and blend until thoroughly mixed.

3 When ready to serve, assemble tacos in tortillas by adding crabmeat, a pinch of baby arugula and sprouts, then top with apricot cocktail sauce. Fasten taco together with toothpicks.

4 Serve cold.

TIP

The apricot cocktail sauce also makes an excellent spread for sandwiches and can be used as a dipping sauce.

FISH TACOS
WITH CITRUS PINEAPPLE SALSA

- 2 cups shredded red cabbage
- 1 jar (16 ounces) Pace® Citrus Pineapple Salsa
- 1¼ pounds cod **or** tilapia
- 1 teaspoon ground cumin
- 1 tablespoon olive oil
- 8 flour tortillas **or** corn tortillas (6-inch), warmed
- 1 cup cotija cheese **or** feta cheese
- ¼ cup chopped fresh cilantro

1 Stir the cabbage and ½ **cup** salsa in a medium bowl. Season the fish with the cumin.

2 Heat the oil in a 12-inch skillet over medium-high heat. Add the fish and cook for 3 minutes per side or until the fish flakes easily when tested with a fork. Add ½ **cup** salsa. Break the fish pieces up with a fork and stir to coat.

3 Spoon about ⅓ **cup** fish mixture into each tortilla. Top **each** with **about ¼ cup** cabbage mixture and **2 tablespoons** cheese. Top with the remaining salsa. Sprinkle with the cilantro and fold the tortillas around the filling.

FISHIN'
FOR TACOS

12 frozen fish sticks
   (8 ounces total)

3 tablespoons salsa

2 tablespoons mayonnaise

4 (8-inch) flour tortillas,
  warmed

1 cup shredded lettuce

½ cup (2 ounces) shredded
  Cheddar cheese

⅓ cup grape tomatoes,
  quartered

1 Bake fish sticks according to package directions.

2 Mix salsa and mayonnaise in small bowl.

3 Place 3 fish sticks in each tortilla. Top evenly with salsa mixture, lettuce, cheese and tomatoes. Roll up tortillas. Serve immediately.

SHRIMP TACOS

- 1 pound jumbo or colossal raw shrimp, peeled and deveined (16 count)
- 2 tablespoons fresh lemon juice, divided
- ½ teaspoon ground cumin, divided
- ¼ teaspoon black pepper
- 1 pint cherry or grape tomatoes, halved
- 1 small red onion, finely chopped
- 1 serrano chile pepper, cored, seeded and minced
- 1 clove garlic, minced
- 1 tablespoon chopped fresh cilantro
- ¼ teaspoon salt
- 1 cup coarsely shredded romaine lettuce
- 1 small avocado, cut into 8 wedges
- 8 (6-inch) corn tortillas or taco shells, heated
  Lime wedges (optional)

1 Cut shrimp along the vein to butterfly. Place in large glass bowl with 1 tablespoon lemon juice, ¼ teaspoon cumin and black pepper; stir to blend. Let stand 30 minutes.

2 Meanwhile, for salsa, combine tomatoes, onion, serrano pepper, garlic, cilantro, remaining 1 tablespoon lemon juice, remaining ¼ teaspoon cumin and salt in small bowl; stir to blend. Set aside.

3 Spray large skillet with nonstick cooking spray; heat over medium heat 30 seconds. Cook shrimp in batches (do not crowd pan) 3 to 4 minutes on each side or until cooked through.

4 Divide shrimp, salsa, lettuce and avocado evenly among tortillas. Serve remaining salsa on the side. Garnish with lime wedges.

FISH TACOS

1 to 1½ pounds firm-fleshed fish fillets, such as red snapper, cut into 4×2-inch strips

2 canned chipotle peppers in adobo sauce, finely chopped

Juice of 2 limes

2 tablespoons chili powder

1 clove garlic, minced

½ teaspoon salt

½ teaspoon black pepper

¼ cup olive oil

½ head red cabbage, shredded

Juice of 1 lemon

½ cup Lime-Cilantro Cream (recipe follows)

½ head red cabbage, shredded

8 to 10 (6-inch) flour tortillas

1 cup queso fresco* or feta cheese, crumbled

Queso fresco is a fresh, white Mexican cheese that is available in Latin markets and some large supermarkets.

1 Place fish, skin side down, in shallow bowl. Combine chipotle peppers, lime juice, chili powder, garlic, salt and black pepper in small bowl. Whisk in oil; pour mixture over fish. Cover; refrigerate 1 hour.

2 Meanwhile, combine cabbage and lemon juice in medium bowl. Toss to coat. Prepare Lime-Cilantro Cream.

3 Prepare grill for direct cooking. Oil grid.

4 Grill fish, skin side up, 4 to 5 minutes. Turn fish; grill 4 to 5 minutes or until center is opaque. Remove to plate; let stand 5 minutes. Remove skin from fish; gently break fish into flakes with fork.

5 Place about ¼ cup fish in center of each tortilla. Top with ¼ cup cabbage, 2 or 3 teaspoons of cheese and ½ teaspoon Lime-Cilantro Cream.

LIME-CILANTRO CREAM

Juice of 2 limes

½ cup fresh cilantro leaves

¼ cup sour cream

Place juice and cilantro in blender; blend 1 minute or until cilantro is minced. Add sour cream; blend until smooth.

SPICY FISH TACOS WITH FRESH SALSA

- ¾ cup plus 2 tablespoons **FRANK'S® RedHot®** Original Cayenne Pepper Sauce, divided
- 1 pound thick, firm white fish fillets, such as cod, halibut or sea bass, cut into ¾-inch cubes
- ½ cup sour cream
- 1½ cups finely chopped plum tomatoes
- ¼ cup minced cilantro
- 2 tablespoons minced red onion
- 8 taco shells, warmed
- 2 cups shredded lettuce

POUR ½ cup **FRANK'S RedHot** Original Cayenne Pepper Sauce over fish in resealable food storage plastic bag or bowl. Marinate in refrigerator 30 minutes.

COMBINE ¼ cup **FRANK'S RedHot** Original Cayenne Pepper Sauce and sour cream in small bowl; chill until needed.

COMBINE tomatoes, cilantro, onion and remaining 2 tablespoons **FRANK'S RedHot** Original Cayenne Pepper Sauce. Reserve.

REMOVE fish from marinade. Spray large nonstick skillet with nonstick cooking spray and heat over medium heat until hot. Stir-fry fish 3 to 5 minutes until just opaque and flakes with fork. Fill each taco shell with shredded lettuce, cooked fish and salsa. Drizzle with sour cream mixture.

VARIATION

Substitute *1 pound* peeled and deveined shrimp for fish.

FISH TACOS
WITH YOGURT SAUCE

SAUCE

- ½ cup plain yogurt
- ¼ cup chopped fresh cilantro
- 3 tablespoons sour cream
  Juice of 1 lime
- 1 tablespoon mayonnaise
- ½ teaspoon ground cumin
- ¼ teaspoon ground red pepper
  Salt and black pepper

TACOS

- Juice of ½ lime
- 2 tablespoons canola oil
- 1½ pounds swordfish, halibut or tilapia fillets
  Salt and black pepper
- 12 (6-inch) corn or flour tortillas
- 3 cups shredded cabbage or prepared coleslaw mixture
- 2 medium tomatoes, chopped

1 For sauce, mix yogurt, cilantro, sour cream, lime juice, mayonnaise, cumin and red pepper in small bowl. Season with salt and black pepper to taste.

2 For tacos, preheat grill or broiler. Combine juice of ½ lime and oil in small bowl. Brush or spoon lime and oil mixture over fish fillets about 5 minutes before cooking. Season with salt and black pepper. (Do not marinate fish longer than about 5 minutes, or acid in lime will begin to "cook" fish.)

3 If grilling fish, spray grid or grill basket with nonstick cooking spray. Prepare grill for direct cooking. Place fish on grid over high heat. Grill, covered 10 minutes, turning once. If broiling fish, spray broiler pan with cooking spray. Broil 4 inches from heat 5 minutes; turn and broil 5 minutes or until center is opaque. Remove from broiler. Flake fish or break into large pieces.

4 Place tortillas on grill or on burner over medium heat. Grill 10 seconds on each side or until beginning to bubble and brown lightly. Fill tortillas with fish. Top with sauce, cabbage and tomatoes.

TINY SHRIMP TACOS
WITH PEACH SALSA

MAKES 24 MINI TACOS

1 peach, peeled and finely diced

2 tablespoons finely chopped red onion

1 jalapeño pepper, finely chopped

Juice of 1 lime

1 tablespoon chopped fresh cilantro or Italian parsley

1 clove garlic, minced

½ teaspoon salt

8 (6-inch) flour tortillas

1 tablespoon vegetable oil

1 pound medium raw shrimp, peeled, deveined and chopped

2 teaspoons chili powder

1 Combine peach, onion, jalapeño, lime juice, cilantro, garlic and salt in medium glass bowl. Set aside.

2 Preheat oven to 400°F. Cut out 24 rounds from tortillas with 2½-inch biscuit cutter or sharp knife. Discard scraps. Drape tortilla rounds over handle of wooden spoon; secure with toothpicks. Bake 5 minutes; repeat with remaining tortilla rounds.

3 Heat oil in large nonstick skillet over medium-high heat. Add shrimp and chili powder; cook and stir 3 minutes or until shrimp are pink and opaque.

4 Place shrimp in taco shells; top with peach salsa.

SEAFOOD TACOS
WITH FRUIT SALSA

2 tablespoons lemon juice

1 teaspoon chili powder

1 teaspoon ground allspice

1 teaspoon olive oil

1 teaspoon minced garlic

1 to 2 teaspoons grated lemon peel

½ teaspoon ground cloves

1 pound halibut or snapper fillets

Fruit Salsa (recipe follows)

12 (6-inch) corn tortillas *or* 6 (7- to 8-inch) flour tortillas

3 cups shredded romaine lettuce

1 small red onion, halved and thinly sliced

Fruit Salsa (recipe follows)

1 Combine lemon juice, chili powder, allspice, oil, garlic, lemon peel and cloves in small bowl; stir to blend. Rub fish with spice mixture; cover and refrigerate while grill heats. (Fish may be cut into smaller pieces for easier handling.)

2 Prepare Fruit Salsa. Spray grid with nonstick cooking spray. Adjust grid 4 to 6 inches above heat. Preheat grill to medium-high heat. Grill fish, covered, 3 minutes or until fish is lightly browned on bottom. Carefully turn fish over; grill 2 minutes or until fish is opaque in center. Remove from heat. Cut into 12 pieces, removing bones if necessary. Cover to keep warm.

3 Place tortillas on grill in single layer and heat 5 to 10 seconds; turn and cook 5 to 10 seconds or until hot and pliable. Stack; cover to keep warm.

4 Top each tortilla with ¼ cup lettuce and red onion. Top fish with about 2 tablespoons Fruit Salsa.

FRUIT SALSA

1 small ripe papaya, peeled, seeded and diced

1 firm small banana, diced

2 green onions, minced

3 tablespoons chopped fresh cilantro or mint

3 tablespoons lime juice

2 jalapeño peppers, seeded and minced

Combine papaya, banana, green onions, cilantro, lime juice and jalapeños in small bowl; stir to blend. Serve at room temperature.

SWEET AND SPICY SHRIMP TACOS
WITH MANGO SALSA

Mango Salsa (recipe follows)
1½ pounds uncooked shrimp, peeled and deveined
1 teaspoon salt
1 teaspoon granulated sugar
½ cup cola beverage
⅓ cup chili sauce
2 tablespoons packed brown sugar
1 tablespoon lime juice
1 teaspoon hot pepper sauce
1 tablespoon chopped fresh cilantro
6 (6-inch) lightly grilled flour tortillas

1 Prepare Mango Salsa.

2 Place shrimp in medium bowl; sprinkle with salt and granulated sugar. Stir to coat; refrigerate 30 minutes.

3 Meanwhile, heat cola, chili sauce, brown sugar, lime juice and hot pepper sauce in small skillet over medium heat until sauce begins to simmer and thicken. Remove from heat. Stir in cilantro. Set aside.

4 Cook shrimp in large skillet over medium-high heat 3 minutes or until shrimp are pink and opaque.

5 Drizzle sauce over cooked shrimp. Serve in flour tortillas topped with Mango Salsa.

MANGO SALSA

2 mangoes, pitted and chopped
1 cucumber, peeled, seeded and chopped
1 red or yellow bell pepper, seeded and chopped
1 jalapeño pepper, seeded and finely chopped
¼ cup diced red onion
1 clove garlic, minced
2 tablespoons chopped fresh cilantro
1 tablespoon lime juice
1 tablespoon cola beverage
Salt and black pepper

Combine mangoes, cucumber, bell pepper, jalapeño pepper, onion, garlic, cilantro, lime juice, cola, salt and black pepper in medium bowl; stir until well combined. Cover; refrigerate 1 to 4 hours before serving.

JERK FISH TACOS

½ cup chopped peeled fresh mango (about ½ medium mango)

½ cup canned black beans, rinsed and drained

1 tablespoon chopped fresh parsley

1 tablespoon sliced green onion

1 tablespoon finely chopped seeded jalapeño pepper (optional)

1 tablespoon frozen orange juice concentrate

1 teaspoon olive oil

2½ teaspoons Jamaican jerk seasoning

1 pound fresh or thawed frozen halibut steaks, cut 1 inch thick

4 (8-inch) flour tortillas, warmed

4 leaves romaine lettuce

1 Preheat broiler. Combine mango, beans, parsley, green onion, jalapeño, if desired, and orange juice concentrate in small bowl. Set aside.

2 Rub oil and jerk seasoning on both sides of fish. Place on rack of broiler pan. Broil 8 to 12 minutes or until fish begins to flake when tested with fork, turning once. Remove and discard skin and bones. Break fish into large bite-size pieces.

3 Fill tortillas with fish, mango mixture and lettuce.

BEEF & PORK TACOS

TACOS
WITH CARNITAS

2 pounds pork leg, shoulder or roast, trimmed of fat

1 medium onion, quartered

3 bay leaves

2 tablespoons chili powder

1 tablespoon dried oregano

1 teaspoon ground cumin
   Salsa Cruda

16 (6-inch) corn tortillas, warmed

4 cups shredded romaine lettuce

1 cup crumbled feta cheese (optional)

1 can (4 ounces) diced mild green chiles

1 Combine pork, onion, bay leaves, chili powder, oregano and cumin in large saucepan or Dutch oven. Add enough water to cover pork. Cover; bring to a boil. Reduce heat to medium-low. Simmer 3 hours or until pork is fork-tender. Meanwhile, prepare Salsa Cruda.

2 Preheat oven to 450°F. Remove pork to large baking dish. Bake 20 minutes or until browned and crisp.

3 Meanwhile, skim fat from cooking liquid. Bring to a boil over high heat. Boil 20 minutes or until reduced to about 1 cup. Remove and discard bay leaves.

4 When cool enough to handle, shred pork with two forks. Add to saucepan; stir to coat. Cover and simmer 10 minutes or until most liquid is absorbed. Remove pork to medium bowl using slotted spoon; discard liquid.

5 Top each tortilla evenly with lettuce, pork, feta cheese, chiles and Salsa Cruda.

SALSA CRUDA

1 cup chopped tomato

2 tablespoons minced onion

2 tablespoons minced fresh cilantro

2 tablespoons lime juice

½ jalapeño pepper, seeded and minced

1 clove garlic, minced

Combine tomato, onion, cilantro, lime juice, jalapeño and garlic in small bowl; gently mix.

SPICY BEEF TACOS

1 pound boneless beef chuck, cut into 1-inch cubes

Vegetable oil

1 to 2 teaspoons chili powder

1 clove garlic, minced

½ teaspoon salt

½ teaspoon ground cumin

1 can (about 14 ounces) diced tomatoes, undrained

12 taco shells or (6-inch) corn tortillas

1 cup (4 ounces) shredded mild Cheddar cheese

2 to 3 cups shredded iceberg lettuce

1 large fresh tomato, seeded and chopped

Chopped fresh cilantro (optional)

1 Brown beef in 2 tablespoons hot oil in large skillet over medium-high heat 10 to 12 minutes, turning frequently. Reduce heat to low. Stir in chili powder, garlic, salt and cumin; cook and stir 30 seconds.

2 Add diced tomatoes with juice; bring to a boil over high heat. Reduce heat to low. Cover and simmer 1½ to 2 hours or until beef is very tender.

3 Using two forks, pull beef into coarse shreds in skillet. Increase heat to medium. Cook, uncovered, 10 to 15 minutes or until most of liquid has evaporated. Keep warm.

4 Fill taco shells with beef, cheese, lettuce and chopped tomato. Garnish with cilantro.

SIMPLE SHREDDED PORK TACOS

- 2 pounds boneless pork roast
- 1 cup salsa
- 1 can (4 ounces) diced mild green chiles, drained
- ½ teaspoon garlic salt
- ½ teaspoon black pepper
- 6 taco shells or (6-inch) corn tortillas

Optional toppings: fresh cooked corn off the cob, sliced mini sweet red peppers, sliced red cabbage, avocado, chopped fresh tomato and/or chopped fresh cilantro

SLOW COOKER DIRECTIONS

1 Combine pork, salsa, chiles, garlic salt and black pepper in slow cooker; stir to blend.

2 Cover; cook on LOW 8 hours. Remove pork to large cutting board; shred with two forks. Stir shredded pork back into slow cooker to keep warm. Serve in taco shells with desired toppings.

DOUBLE DECKER TACOS

2 tablespoons all-purpose flour
2 teaspoons chili powder
1 teaspoon dried minced onion
¾ teaspoon paprika
½ teaspoon salt
½ teaspoon garlic powder
¼ teaspoon sugar
1 pound ground beef
⅔ cup water
8 taco shells
8 mini (5-inch) flour tortillas*
2 cups refried beans, warmed
2 cups shredded romaine lettuce
1 cup chopped tomato
1 cup (4 ounces) shredded Cheddar cheese
Sour cream (optional)

Mini flour tortillas may also be labeled as street tacos.

1 Preheat oven to 350°F. Combine flour, chili powder, onion, paprika, salt, garlic powder and sugar in small bowl; mix well.

2 Brown beef in large skillet over medium-high heat 6 to 8 minutes or until browned, stirring to break up meat. Drain fat. Add flour mixture; cook and stir 2 minutes. Stir in water; bring to a simmer. Reduce heat to medium. Cook 10 minutes or until most liquid has evaporated. Meanwhile, heat taco shells in oven 5 minutes or until warm.

3 Wrap tortillas in damp paper towel; microwave on HIGH 25 to 35 seconds or until warm. Spread each tortilla with ¼ cup refried beans, leaving ¼-inch border around edge. Wrap flour tortillas around outside of taco shells, pressing gently to seal together.

4 Fill taco shells with beef mixture; top with lettuce, tomato and cheese. Drizzle with sour cream, if desired. Serve immediately.

TOMATILLO PORK TACOS

2 teaspoons canola oil

1 pound pork tenderloin, cut into ½-inch pieces

1 teaspoon ground cumin

1 teaspoon chili powder

½ cup chopped onion

3 cloves garlic, minced (optional)

¾ cup tomatillo salsa, divided

8 (6-inch) flour or corn tortillas

1 cup diced ripe tomato

1 cup shredded romaine lettuce

½ cup (2 ounces) shredded 2% milk Mexican cheese blend or crumbled queso fresco cheese

1 Heat oil in large nonstick skillet over medium heat. Add pork, cumin and chili powder; stir until pork is coated with spices. Add onion and garlic, if desired; cook and stir 5 minutes or until pork is no longer pink. Add ½ cup salsa; simmer 4 minutes or until pork is cooked through.

2 Wrap tortillas loosely in waxed paper and heat in microwave oven at MEDIUM (50%) 30 seconds or until warmed.

3 Serve pork mixture in tortillas topped with tomato, lettuce, cheese and remaining ¼ cup salsa.

PICADILLO TACOS

6 ounces ground beef

½ cup chopped green bell pepper

½ teaspoon ground cumin

½ teaspoon chili powder

⅛ teaspoon ground cinnamon

½ cup chunky salsa

1 tablespoon golden raisins

4 (6-inch) corn tortillas, warmed

½ cup shredded lettuce

¼ cup (1 ounce) shredded Cheddar cheese

1 small tomato, chopped

1 Heat large nonstick skillet over medium heat. Add beef, bell pepper, cumin, chili powder and cinnamon; cook and stir 6 to 8 minutes until meat is browned. Stir in salsa and raisins. Reduce heat to low. Simmer 5 minutes or until meat is cooked through, stirring occasionally.

2 Divide meat mixture evenly among tortillas. Top with lettuce, cheese and tomato.

SLOW-COOKED TACO SHREDDED BEEF

1 can (10¾ ounces)
   Campbell's® Condensed
   French Onion Soup

1 tablespoon chili powder

½ teaspoon ground cumin

2 pounds boneless beef chuck
   roast

2 tablespoons finely chopped
   fresh cilantro leaves

16 taco shells

1 cup shredded Cheddar
   cheese (about 4 ounces)

   Shredded lettuce

   Sour cream

SLOW COOKER DIRECTIONS

1 Stir the soup, chili powder and cumin in a 4-quart slow cooker. Add the beef and turn to coat.

2 Cover and cook on LOW for 6 to 7 hours* or until the beef is fork-tender.

3 Remove the beef from the cooker to a cutting board and let stand for 10 minutes. Using 2 forks, shred the beef. Return the beef to the cooker. Stir the cilantro in the cooker.

4 Spoon **about ¼ cup** beef mixture into **each** taco shell. Top **each** with **about 1 tablespoon** cheese. Top with the lettuce and the sour cream.

Or on HIGH for 4 to 5 hours.

CARNITAS TACOS

1½ pounds boneless pork loin, cut into 1-inch cubes

1 onion, finely chopped

½ cup chicken broth

1 tablespoon chili powder

2 teaspoons ground cumin

1 teaspoon dried oregano

½ teaspoon minced canned chipotle pepper in adobo sauce (optional)

½ cup pico de gallo

2 tablespoons chopped fresh cilantro

½ teaspoon salt

12 (6-inch) corn tortillas

¾ cup (3 ounces) shredded sharp Cheddar cheese

3 tablespoons sour cream

SLOW COOKER DIRECTIONS

1 Combine pork, onion, broth, chili powder, cumin, oregano and chipotle pepper, if desired, in slow cooker. Cover; cook on LOW 6 hours or on HIGH 3 hours or until pork is very tender. Pour off excess cooking liquid.

2 Shred pork with two forks; stir in pico de gallo, cilantro and salt. Cover and keep warm.

3 Cut three circles from each tortilla with 2-inch biscuit cutter. Top with pork, cheese and sour cream.

TIP

Carnitas means "little meats" in Spanish. This dish is usually made with an inexpensive cut of pork that is simmered for a long time until it falls to pieces. The meat is then browned in pork fat. The slow cooker makes the long, slow cooking process easy to manage and skipping the final browning lowers the fat content.

NACHO TACOS

1 pound ground beef

1 medium onion, chopped
   (about ½ cup)

½ teaspoon chili powder

1 can (10¾ ounces)
   Campbell's® Condensed
   Fiesta Nacho Cheese Soup

8 taco shells, warmed

1 cup shredded lettuce

1 medium tomato, chopped
   (about 1 cup)

1 Cook the beef, onion and chili powder in a 10-inch skillet over medium-high heat until the beef is well browned, stirring often to separate the meat. Pour off any fat.

2 Stir ½ **cup** soup in the skillet and cook until the mixture is hot and bubbling.

3 Heat the remaining soup in a 1-quart saucepan over medium-high heat until hot and bubbling. Spoon the beef mixture into the taco shells. Top with the soup, lettuce and tomato.

SHREDDED CHIPOTLE PORK TACOS WITH ROASTED GREEN ONIONS

MAKES 16 TACOS

6 cups water

2 pounds boneless pork shoulder roast, cut into 2-inch pieces

1 medium onion, thinly sliced

¼ cup cider vinegar, divided

1 teaspoon salt

1 tablespoon olive oil

1 cup finely chopped onion

4 cloves garlic, minced

1 can (about 8 ounces) tomato sauce

3 chipotle peppers in adobo sauce, finely chopped and mashed with a fork

½ teaspoon ground cumin

Roasted Green Onions (recipe follows)

16 (6-inch) corn tortillas

1 Bring water to a boil in Dutch oven over high heat. Add pork, sliced onion, 3 tablespoons vinegar and salt; return to a boil. Reduce heat; simmer, partially covered, 1½ hours. Remove pork with slotted spoon to large cutting board and cool slightly; reserve 1 cup cooking liquid. Shred pork with two forks; set aside.

2 Heat oil in large nonstick skillet over medium-high heat. Add chopped onion; cook and stir 3 minutes. Add garlic; cook 15 seconds. Add tomato sauce, chipotles, cumin, remaining 1 tablespoon vinegar, shredded pork and reserved cooking liquid; cook and stir 2 minutes or until heated through. Remove from heat. Cover; let stand 10 minutes.

3 Meanwhile, prepare Roasted Green Onions. Heat tortillas over stovetop burner or grill about 15 seconds per side or until lightly charred. Fill each tortilla evenly with pork mixture and Roasted Green Onions.

ROASTED GREEN ONIONS

Preheat oven to 425°F. Trim 16 green onions; place on large baking sheet. Drizzle with 2 teaspoons olive oil; toss gently to coat. Arrange in single layer and bake 10 minutes. Sprinkle with salt.

SPEEDY TACOS

4 ounces ground beef sirloin

½ cup chopped onion, divided

1 clove garlic, minced

⅓ cup tomato sauce

1 tablespoon taco seasoning mix

6 taco shells

¼ cup (2 ounces) shredded Cheddar cheese

½ cup shredded lettuce

⅓ cup chopped tomato

Hot pepper sauce (optional)

1 Heat small skillet over medium heat. Add beef, ¼ cup chopped onion and garlic; cook and stir 5 minutes or until beef is browned, breaking up meat with spoon. Add tomato sauce and taco seasoning mix; cook 5 minutes.

2 Warm taco shells in oven following package directions.

3 Fill taco shells with beef mixture, cheese, lettuce, tomato and remaining ¼ cup chopped onion. Serve with hot pepper sauce, if desired.

SPICY SHREDDED BEEF TACOS

1 boneless beef chuck roast
    (2½ pounds)

1¼ teaspoons salt, divided

1 teaspoon *each* ground
    cumin, garlic powder and
    smoked paprika

2 tablespoons olive oil, divided

2 cups beef broth

1 red bell pepper, sliced

1 tomato, cut into wedges

½ onion, sliced

2 cloves garlic, minced

1 to 2 canned chipotle peppers
    in adobo sauce

    Juice of 1 lime

6 (6-inch) corn or flour tortillas

    Optional toppings: sliced bell
    peppers, avocado, diced
    onion, lime wedges and/or
    chopped fresh cilantro

SLOW COOKER DIRECTIONS

1 Season beef with 1 teaspoon salt, cumin, garlic powder and smoked paprika. Heat 1 tablespoon oil in large skillet over medium-high heat. Add beef; cook 5 minutes on each side until browned. Remove to slow cooker.

2 Pour in broth. Cover; cook on LOW 8 to 9 hours or on HIGH 4 to 5 hours.

3 Meanwhile, preheat oven to 425°F. Combine bell pepper, tomato, onion and garlic on large baking sheet. Drizzle with remaining 1 tablespoon oil. Roast 40 minutes or until vegetables are tender. Place vegetables, chipotle pepper, lime juice and remaining ¼ teaspoon salt in food processor or blender; blend until smooth.

4 Remove beef to large cutting board; shred with two forks. Combine shredded meat with 1 cup cooking liquid. Discard remaining cooking liquid. Serve on tortillas with sauce. Top as desired.

ANCHO CHILE AND LIME PORK TACOS

2 large plantain leaves
1 pork shoulder roast
   (4 to 6 pounds)*
   Juice of 4 to 5 medium limes
1 package (about 1 ounce)
   ancho chile paste
   Salt
1 large onion, sliced
   Pickled Red Onions (recipe
   follows)
   Cilantro-Lime Rice (optional)
10 (6-inch) flour tortillas
   Lime slices (optional)

Unless you have a 5-, 6- or 7-quart slow cooker, cut any roast larger than 2½ pounds in half so it cooks completely.

SLOW COOKER DIRECTIONS

1 Line slow cooker with plantain leaves; top with pork roast. Combine lime juice, chile paste and salt in medium bowl; stir until well blended. Add paste mixture and onion to slow cooker; wrap leaves over pork. Cover; cook on LOW 8 to 10 hours.

2 Meanwhile, prepare Pickled Red Onions and Cilantro-Lime Rice, if desired.

3 Serve pork in tortillas; top with Pickled Red Onions. Serve with lime slices and Cilantro-Lime Rice, if desired.

PICKLED RED ONIONS

Combine 1 cup sliced red onion and juice from 1 to 2 limes in small bowl; set aside until juice is absorbed. Makes 1 cup.

CILANTRO-LIME RICE

Prepare rice according to package directions. Add 2 to 4 tablespoons butter, ¼ to ½ cup chopped fresh cilantro, juice of 2 to 4 medium limes and ½ to 1 teaspoon salt. Makes 10 to 12 servings.

CONEY ISLAND CHILI DOG TACOS

1 tablespoon olive oil

8 hot dogs

1¼ pounds 90% extra lean ground beef

1 tablespoon chili powder

1 jar (16 ounces) Pace® Chunky Salsa-Mild

8 flour tortillas (6-inch) **or** taco shells, warmed

1 medium onion, diced (about ½ cup)

½ cup shredded Cheddar cheese

1 Heat the oil in a 12-inch skillet over medium-high heat. Add the hot dogs and cook until browned. Remove the hot dogs, cover and keep warm.

2 Cook the beef and chili powder in the skillet until the beef is well browned, stirring often to separate meat. Pour off any fat. Stir in the salsa. Reduce the heat to low. Cook for 5 minutes, stirring occasionally.

3 Place 1 hot dog into each tortilla. Top with the beef mixture, onion and cheese.

PREP AHEAD

You can prepare the beef mixture, cool it completely, then place into a resealable freezer bag (remove all air), seal the bag and refrigerate for up to 3 days. Or, freeze for up to 3 months and thaw overnight in the refrigerator before reheating. Reheat in the skillet after cooking the hot dogs as shown.

SERVING SUGGESTION

Try topping these chili dogs with a drizzle of yellow mustard.

SOFT TACOS

1 pound ground beef

1 package (about 1 ounce) taco seasoning mix

¾ cup water

8 flour tortillas (8-inch), warmed

1 cup Pace® Picante Sauce

1 cup shredded lettuce

1 cup shredded Cheddar cheese

SLOW COOKER DIRECTIONS

1 Cook the beef in a 10-inch skillet over medium-high heat until the beef is well browned, stirring often to separate the meat. Pour off any fat.

2 Stir the taco seasoning mix and water in the skillet and heat to a boil. Reduce the heat to low and cook for 5 minutes, stirring occasionally.

3 Spoon **about ¼ cup** beef mixture down the center of **each** tortilla. Top **each** with **about 2 tablespoons** picante sauce, lettuce and cheese. Fold the tortilla around the filling. Serve with additional picante sauce.

CHICKEN & TURKEY TACOS

CHICKEN AND SPICY BLACK BEAN TACOS

1 can (about 15 ounces) black beans, rinsed and drained

1 can (10 ounces) diced tomatoes with mild green chiles, drained

1½ teaspoons chili powder

¾ teaspoon ground cumin

1 tablespoon plus 1 teaspoon extra virgin olive oil, divided

12 ounces boneless skinless chicken breasts

12 crisp corn taco shells

Optional toppings: shredded lettuce, diced fresh tomatoes, shredded cheese, sour cream and/or sliced pitted black olives

SLOW COOKER DIRECTIONS

1 Coat inside of slow cooker with nonstick cooking spray. Add beans and tomatoes with chiles. Blend chili powder, cumin and 1 teaspoon oil in small bowl; rub onto chicken. Place chicken in slow cooker. Cover; cook on HIGH 1¾ hours.

2 Remove chicken to large cutting board; slice. Remove bean mixture to bowl using slotted spoon. Stir in remaining 1 tablespoon oil.

3 To serve, warm taco shells according to package directions. Fill with equal amounts of bean mixture and chicken. Top as desired.

SOFT TURKEY TACOS

8 (6-inch) corn or flour tortillas
1½ teaspoons vegetable oil
1 pound ground turkey
1 small onion, chopped
1 teaspoon dried oregano
Salt and black pepper
Chopped tomatoes
Shredded lettuce
Salsa

1 Wrap tortillas in foil. Place in cold oven; set temperature to 350°F.

2 Heat oil in large skillet over medium heat. Add turkey and onion; cook 6 to 8 minutes or until turkey is no longer pink, stirring occasionally. Stir in oregano. Season with salt and pepper.

3 For each taco, fill warm tortilla with turkey mixture. Top with tomatoes, lettuce and salsa.

NOTE

To warm tortillas in microwave oven, wrap loosely in damp paper towel. Microwave on HIGH 2 minutes.

SHREDDED CHICKEN TACOS

2 pounds boneless skinless chicken thighs

½ cup mango salsa, plus additional for serving

Lettuce (optional)

8 (6-inch) yellow corn tortillas, warmed

SLOW COOKER DIRECTIONS

1 Coat inside of slow cooker with nonstick cooking spray. Add chicken and ½ cup salsa. Cover; cook on LOW 4 to 5 hours or on HIGH 2½ to 3 hours.

2 Remove chicken to large cutting board; shred with two forks. Stir shredded chicken back into slow cooker. Divide chicken and lettuce, if desired, evenly among tortillas. Serve with additional salsa.

TUESDAY NIGHT TACOS

1 tablespoon vegetable oil

1½ pounds boneless skinless chicken thighs

1 cup chunky salsa

6 (6-inch) corn tortillas, warmed

½ cup shredded lettuce

1 cup pico de gallo

1 cup (4 ounces) shredded taco blend or Cheddar cheese (optional)

Lime wedges (optional)

Optional toppings: sour cream, sliced jalapeño peppers, pickled onions and/or avocado

1 Heat oil in large skillet. Add chicken; cook 10 to 12 minutes or until cooked through. Add salsa; cook 1 minute, scraping up browned bits from bottom of skillet. Turn chicken to coat with salsa. Remove chicken to large cutting board; shred with two forks.

2 Serve chicken mixture in tortillas with lettuce, pico de gallo, cheese and lime wedges, if desired. Top as desired.

TURKEY TACOS

1 pound ground turkey

1 medium onion, chopped

1 can (6 ounces) tomato paste

½ cup chunky salsa

1 tablespoon chopped fresh cilantro

¾ teaspoon salt, divided

1 tablespoon butter

1 tablespoon all-purpose flour

⅓ cup milk

½ cup sour cream

Ground red pepper

8 taco shells

SLOW COOKER DIRECTIONS

1 Heat large skillet over medium heat. Add turkey and onion; cook 6 to 8 minutes or until turkey is no longer pink, stirring to separate meat. Drain. Remove turkey mixture to slow cooker.

2 Add tomato paste, salsa, cilantro and ½ teaspoon salt to slow cooker. Cover; cook on LOW 4 to 5 hours.

3 Just before serving, melt butter in small saucepan over low heat. Stir in flour and remaining ¼ teaspoon salt; cook 1 minute. Gradually stir in milk. Cook and stir over low heat until thickened. Remove from heat.

4 Combine sour cream and ground red pepper in small bowl. Stir into hot milk mixture. Return to heat. Cook over low heat 1 minute, stirring constantly.

5 Spoon ¼ cup turkey mixture into each taco shell; keep warm. Spoon sour cream mixture over taco filling.

CAJUN CHICKEN TACOS

1 pound skinless, boneless chicken breast halves, cubed

1 tablespoon Cajun seasoning

1 tablespoon olive oil

1 cup Pace® Chunky Salsa-Mild

2 stalks celery, chopped (about ½ cup)

1 medium red bell pepper, finely chopped (about ½ cup)

1 can (about 15 ounces) kidney beans, rinsed and drained

½ cup sour cream

8 flour tortillas (6-inch), warmed

1 Season the chicken with the Cajun seasoning. Heat the oil in a 12-inch skillet over medium-high heat. Add the chicken and cook for 7 minutes or until well browned and cooked through, stirring occasionally. Stir in ½ cup salsa, the celery, pepper and beans and cook until hot.

2 Divide the chicken mixture, sour cream and remaining ½ cup salsa among the tortillas. Fold the tortillas around the filling.

PREP AHEAD

To save on prep at dinnertime, you can cut up the celery and bell pepper and store in resealable bags in the refrigerator for up to 3 days.

TURKEY AND WINTER SQUASH TACOS

4 crisp corn taco shells

2 teaspoons vegetable oil

¼ cup finely chopped onion

1 cup diced cooked butternut or delicata squash

1 teaspoon taco seasoning mix

1 cup chopped cooked turkey, warmed

Salt and black pepper

¼ cup salsa

1 avocado, cut into 8 thin wedges

1 Preheat oven to 325°F. Place taco shells on baking sheet; heat according to package directions.

2 Meanwhile, heat oil in large skillet over medium-high heat. Add onion; cook and stir 3 minutes. Add squash and taco seasoning mix; cook and stir 2 to 3 minutes.

3 To assemble tacos, place ¼ cup turkey in each taco shell. Season with salt and pepper. Top with squash mixture, 1 tablespoon salsa and 2 slices avocado.

NOTE

Some supermarkets carry packaged diced squash; simply follow the cooking instructions on the package. To use whole squash, peel the squash, cut in half and remove the seeds. Cut the squash into ¾-inch-long strips, then cut crosswise into ¾-inch chunks. Measure 1 cup squash. Heat 1 tablespoon vegetable oil in a medium skillet over medium-low heat. Add the squash; cook and stir 10 to 15 minutes or until fork-tender.

EASY CHICKEN AND RICE TACOS

1 tablespoon butter or margarine

1 pound ground chicken or turkey

1 small onion, chopped

1 packet (1¼ ounces) taco seasoning mix

1¼ cups water

1 can (8 ounces) tomato sauce

1½ cups MINUTE® White Rice, uncooked

1 can (15 ounces) kidney beans, drained and rinsed

16 taco shells, heated

1 package (8 ounces) Cheddar cheese, shredded

1 cup lettuce, shredded

2 medium tomatoes, chopped

Melt butter in large skillet over medium-high heat. Add chicken and onions; cook and stir until chicken is cooked through.

Stir in seasoning mix, water and tomato sauce. Bring to a boil. Reduce heat to low; cover. Simmer 5 minutes.

Add rice and beans; mix well. Cover; remove from heat. Let stand 5 minutes.

Fill taco shells evenly with chicken mixture; top with cheese, lettuce and tomatoes.

GRILLED CHICKEN TACOS

½ cup Pace® Picante Sauce

2 teaspoons lemon juice

2 medium avocados, peeled, pitted and diced

1 medium tomato, chopped (about 1 cup)

2 green onions, sliced (about ¼ cup)

6 skinless, boneless chicken breast halves (about 1½ pounds)

2 tablespoons vegetable oil

12 flour tortillas (8-inch), warmed

3 ounces shredded Cheddar cheese (about ¾ cup)

1 Stir the picante sauce, lemon juice, avocados, tomato and onions in a medium bowl.

2 Brush the chicken with the oil. Lightly oil the grill rack and heat the grill to medium. Grill the chicken for 15 minutes or until it's cooked through, turning once during grilling.

3 Slice the chicken into thin strips and place down center of **each** tortilla. Top with the avocado mixture and the cheese. Roll the tortilla around the filling. Serve with additional picante sauce.

TURKEY TACOS

1 pound turkey breast cutlets,*
   sliced ¼ inch thick

Juice of 1 lime

¼ teaspoon chipotle chili
   powder

1 jalapeño pepper, cored,
   seeded and minced

1 can (about 15 ounces) pinto
   beans, rinsed and drained

¼ teaspoon salt

¼ teaspoon ground cumin

8 corn taco shells

½ cup finely chopped romaine
   lettuce

1 small onion, chopped

¼ cup minced fresh cilantro

¼ cup salsa, drained of excess
   liquid

*Or, you can substitute with
boneless skinless chicken breasts,
sliced to ¼-inch thickness.*

1 Place turkey in shallow glass bowl. Add lime juice and chili powder. Turn to coat turkey. Set aside at room temperature 15 minutes. Coat small skillet with nonstick cooking spray and heat over medium heat. Add jalapeño; cook 1 to 2 minutes to soften. Add beans, salt and cumin; heat through. Set aside.

2 Preheat grill to medium-high heat. Spray grid with cooking spray. Grill turkey 2 minutes per side or until cooked through. Cut into bite-size strips.

3 Heat taco shells, if desired. Divide turkey strips among taco shells. Top each taco with about 1 tablespoon of beans. Sprinkle with lettuce, onion, cilantro and salsa. Serve immediately.

TACOS DORADOS

2 tablespoons vegetable oil

1¾ pounds boneless skinless chicken breasts, cut into 1-inch cubes

½ cup chopped onion

1 can (about 28 ounces) diced tomatoes

2 teaspoons chili powder

1 teaspoon ground cumin

½ teaspoon salt

½ teaspoon garlic powder

½ teaspoon dried oregano

¼ teaspoon ground coriander

10 (8-inch) flour tortillas

3½ cups (14 ounces) shredded queso blanco*

¼ cup chopped fresh cilantro

Salsa and jalapeño peppers

Queso blanco is white Mexican cheese. It is available in most large supermarkets and in Mexican markets.

1 Heat oil in large skillet over medium-high heat. Add chicken; cook and stir until cooked through. Remove from skillet; set aside.

2 Add onion to skillet; cook and stir 5 to 7 minutes or until translucent. Add tomatoes, chili powder, cumin, salt, garlic powder, oregano and coriander; cook and stir 15 minutes or until thickened. Add chicken; mix well.

3 Preheat oven to 450°F. Divide chicken mixture among tortillas; roll up tightly. Place, seam-side down, in 13×9-inch baking dish. Bake 15 minutes or until tortillas are crisp and brown. Sprinkle with queso blanco. Bake 5 minutes or until cheese is melted. Sprinkle with cilantro. Serve with salsa and jalapeños.

QUICK CHICKEN TACOS

MAKES 4 TACOS ▶

1 can (4.5 ounces) Swanson® Premium White Chunk Chicken Breast in Water, drained
¼ cup Pace® Salsa
Shredded lettuce
4 taco shells
Shredded Cheddar cheese
Sour cream

1 Stir the chicken and salsa in a 1-quart saucepan. Heat over low heat until the mixture is hot and bubbling, stirring often.

2 Arrange the lettuce in the taco shells. Top with ¼ **cup** chicken mixture, cheese and sour cream. Serve with additional salsa, if desired.

SALSA VERDE CHICKEN TACOS

MAKES 8 TACOS

1 pound diced skinless, boneless chicken breast halves
1 tablespoon vegetable oil
1 cup Pace® Salsa Verde
1 small avocado, pitted, peeled and diced (about ½ cup)
1 teaspoon lime juice
1 medium red bell pepper, diced (about ½ cup)
½ cup sour cream
8 flour tortillas (6-inch) **or** taco shells, warmed

1 Season the chicken as desired. Heat the oil in a 12-inch skillet over medium-high heat. Add the chicken and cook for 5 minutes or until well browned and cooked through, stirring occasionally. Stir in ½ **cup** salsa verde and cook until hot.

2 Place the avocado into a medium bowl. Add the lime juice and toss to coat.

3 Divide the chicken mixture, pepper, avocado mixture, sour cream and **remaining ½ cup** salsa verde among the tortillas. Fold the tortillas around the filling.

SOFT TACOS
WITH CHICKEN

8 (6- or 7-inch) corn tortillas
2 tablespoons butter
1 medium onion, chopped
1½ cups shredded cooked chicken
1 can (4 ounces) diced mild green chiles, drained
2 tablespoons chopped fresh cilantro
1 cup (½ pint) sour cream
  Salt and black pepper
1½ cups (6 ounces) shredded Monterey Jack cheese
1 large avocado, sliced
  Green taco sauce

1 Stack and wrap tortillas in foil. Warm in 350°F oven 15 minutes or until heated through.

2 Melt butter in large skillet over medium heat. Add onion; cook 6 minutes or until tender. Add chicken, chiles and cilantro; cook 3 minutes or until mixture is heated through. Reduce heat to low. Stir in sour cream; season with salt and pepper. Heat gently; do not boil.

3 To assemble tacos, evenly spoon chicken mixture into center of each tortilla; sprinkle with cheese. Top with avocado and drizzle with taco sauce. Roll tortilla into cone shape or fold in half to eat.

CHICKEN NACHO TACOS

1 tablespoon vegetable oil

1 medium onion, chopped (about ½ cup)

½ teaspoon chili powder

1 can (10¾ ounces) Campbell's® Condensed Fiesta Nacho Cheese Soup

2 cans (4.5 ounces **each**) Swanson® Premium White Chunk Chicken Breast in Water, drained

8 taco shells, warmed

Shredded lettuce

Chopped tomato

1 Heat the oil in a 10-inch skillet over medium-high heat. Add the onion and chili powder and cook until the onion is tender, stirring often.

2 Stir the soup and chicken in the skillet and cook until the mixture is hot and bubbling. Spoon the chicken mixture into the taco shells. Top with the lettuce and tomato.

ON THE SIDE

FRIJOLES BORRACHOS
(DRUNKEN BEANS)

6 slices bacon, chopped

1 medium yellow onion, chopped

1 tablespoon minced garlic

3 jalapeño peppers, seeded and finely diced

1 tablespoon dried oregano

1 can (12 ounces) beer

6 cups water

1 pound dried pinto beans, rinsed and sorted

1 can (about 14 ounces) diced tomatoes

1 tablespoon kosher salt

¼ cup chopped fresh cilantro

SLOW COOKER DIRECTIONS

1 Heat large skillet over medium-high heat. Add bacon; cook 5 minutes or until mostly browned and crisp. Remove to slow cooker. Discard all but 3 tablespoons of drippings.

2 Heat same skillet over medium heat. Add onion; cook 6 minutes or until softened and lightly browned. Add garlic, jalapeños and oregano; cook 30 seconds or until fragrant. Increase heat to medium-high. Add beer; bring to a simmer. Cook 2 minutes, stirring and scraping any brown bits from bottom of skillet. Remove mixture to slow cooker.

3 Add water, beans, tomatoes and salt to slow cooker. Cover; cook on LOW 8 hours or on HIGH 6 hours. Mash beans slightly until broth is thickened and creamy. Stir in cilantro.

MEXICAN RICE OLÉ

1 teaspoon vegetable oil
1 cup uncooked long grain rice
1 teaspoon salt
1 clove garlic, minced
1 can (about 14 ounces) chicken broth
1 can (10¾ ounces) condensed cream of chicken soup, undiluted
¾ cup sour cream
1 can (4 ounces) chopped mild green chiles, undrained
⅓ cup salsa
1 teaspoon ground cumin
1 cup (4 ounces) shredded Cheddar cheese
1 can (about 2 ounces) sliced pitted black olives, drained

1 Preheat oven to 350°F. Spray 3-quart casserole with nonstick cooking spray.

2 Heat oil in large skillet over medium heat. Add rice, salt and garlic; cook and stir 2 to 3 minutes or until rice is well coated. Add enough water to broth to equal 2 cups. Pour into skillet; cook 15 minutes or until rice is tender, stirring occasionally.

3 Remove skillet from heat. Add soup, sour cream, chiles, salsa and cumin; stir to blend. Remove to prepared casserole.

4 Bake 20 minutes. Top with cheese and olives. Bake 5 to 10 minutes or until cheese is melted and casserole is heated through.

JALAPEÑO AND PALE ALE CORN BREAD
WITH HONEY BUTTER

1½ cups all-purpose flour

1½ cups yellow cornmeal

⅓ cup sugar

2 teaspoons baking powder

¾ teaspoon salt

½ teaspoon baking soda

1 cup pale ale

½ cup corn oil

½ cup buttermilk

2 eggs

2 jalapeño peppers, finely chopped

Honey Butter (recipe follows)

1 Preheat oven to 400°F. Butter 8-inch square baking pan.

2 Combine flour, cornmeal, sugar, baking powder, salt and baking soda in large bowl. Combine ale, oil, buttermilk, eggs and jalapeños in medium bowl. Stir ale mixture into flour mixture just until moistened. Pour batter into prepared baking pan.

3 Bake 25 to 27 minutes or until toothpick inserted into center comes out clean. Cool in pan 10 minutes. Prepare Honey Butter.

4 Cut corn bread into squares and serve warm with Honey Butter.

HONEY BUTTER

Combine 6 tablespoons (¾ stick) softened unsalted butter, 2 tablespoons honey and ¼ teaspoon salt in small bowl; stir until smooth.

MEXICAN-STYLE CORN ON THE COB

MAKES 4 SERVINGS ▶

2 tablespoons mayonnaise
½ teaspoon chili powder
½ teaspoon grated lime peel
4 ears corn, shucked
2 tablespoons grated
   Parmesan cheese

1 Prepare grill for direct cooking. Combine mayonnaise, chili powder and lime peel in small bowl; set aside.

2 Grill corn over medium-high heat, uncovered, 4 to 6 minutes or until lightly charred, turning three times. Immediately spread mayonnaise mixture over corn. Sprinkle with cheese.

LIME'D REFRIED BLACK BEANS
WITH VEGGIES AND RICE

MAKES 4 SERVINGS

3 cups cooked quick-cooking brown rice (¾ cup uncooked)
½ cup chopped green onions (white and green parts)
1 medium tomato, seeded and diced, plus additional for topping
¼ cup chopped cilantro, plus additional for topping
2 tablespoons extra virgin olive oil
½ teaspoon salt
1 can (about 15 ounces) black beans, rinsed and drained
½ cup salsa or picante sauce
1 to 2 tablespoons lime juice
⅓ cup sour cream
½ teaspoon ground cumin
1½ cups (6 ounces) shredded Monterey Jack cheese

1 Preheat oven to 350°F. Toss cooked rice with green onions, 1 diced tomato, ¼ cup cilantro, oil and salt. Spread rice mixture evenly in 9-inch deep-dish pie pan; set aside.

2 Place beans, salsa, lime juice, sour cream and cumin in blender or food processor; blend until smooth. Spoon bean mixture evenly over rice mixture; sprinkle evenly with cheese. Bake 20 to 30 minutes or until bubbly around edge and cheese is melted. Top with additional tomatoes and cilantro, if desired. Let stand 10 minutes before serving.

BAKED SPANISH RICE AND BARLEY

2 teaspoons vegetable oil

½ cup chopped onion

½ cup chopped green bell pepper

2 cloves garlic, minced

1 cup coarsely chopped seeded tomatoes

1 cup vegetable broth

½ cup uncooked rice

½ cup water

3 tablespoons quick-cooking barley

¼ teaspoon black pepper

⅛ teaspoon salt

1 Preheat oven to 350°F. Spray 1½-quart baking dish with nonstick cooking spray.

2 Heat oil in medium saucepan over medium heat. Add onion, bell pepper and garlic; cook and stir 5 minutes or until tender. Stir in tomatoes, broth, rice, water, barley, black pepper and salt; bring to a boil over high heat.

3 Pour into prepared baking dish. Cover; bake 25 to 30 minutes or until rice and barley are tender and liquid is absorbed. Fluff with fork.

CHEESY STUFFED POBLANO PEPPERS

3 tablespoons olive oil, divided
1 cup frozen corn, thawed
1 cup diced red onion, divided
¾ cup (3 ounces) crumbled queso blanco cheese
½ cup (2 ounces) shredded Monterey Jack cheese
¼ cup minced fresh cilantro
2 teaspoons minced garlic, divided
4 poblano or green bell peppers
2 medium tomatoes, seeded and diced
Juice of 1 lime
Salt and black pepper

1 Preheat oven to 450°F. Heat 1 tablespoon oil in medium skillet over medium-high heat. Add corn and ½ cup onion; cook and stir 5 minutes. Remove to large bowl. Stir in cheeses, cilantro and 1 teaspoon garlic.

2 Make two long slits on front of each pepper to create flap. Lift flap; remove and discard seeds and ribs. Divide corn mixture evenly among peppers. Replace flap; secure with wooden skewer, if desired. Place stuffed peppers in baking dish. Brush skins with 1 tablespoon oil.

3 Roast peppers 15 to 20 minutes or until peppers are wrinkled and filling is melted. Meanwhile, combine tomatoes, remaining ½ cup onion, lime juice, remaining 1 tablespoon oil, 1 teaspoon garlic, salt and black pepper in medium bowl. Serve tomato mixture with peppers.

SIMMERED RED BEANS
WITH RICE

2 cans (about 15 ounces each) red beans, rinsed and drained

1 can (about 14 ounces) diced tomatoes

½ cup chopped celery

½ cup chopped green bell pepper

½ cup chopped green onions

2 cloves garlic, minced

1 to 2 teaspoons hot pepper sauce

1 teaspoon Worcestershire sauce

1 bay leaf

Hot cooked rice

SLOW COOKER DIRECTIONS

1 Combine beans, tomatoes, celery, bell pepper, green onions, garlic, hot pepper sauce, Worcestershire sauce and bay leaf in slow cooker. Cover; cook on LOW 4 to 6 hours or on HIGH 2 to 3 hours.

2 Slightly mash mixture in slow cooker with potato masher to thicken. Cover; cook on LOW 30 to 60 minutes. Remove and discard bay leaf. Serve over rice.

CHARRED CORN SALAD

3 tablespoons fresh lime juice

½ teaspoon salt

¼ cup extra virgin olive oil

4 to 6 ears corn, husked (enough to make 3 to 4 cups kernels)

⅔ cup canned black beans, rinsed and drained

½ cup chopped fresh cilantro

2 teaspoons minced seeded chipotle pepper (about 1 canned chipotle pepper in adobo sauce)

1 Whisk lime juice and salt in small bowl. Gradually whisk in oil until well blended. Set aside.

2 Cut corn kernels off cobs. Heat large skillet over medium-high heat. Cook corn in single layer 15 to 17 minutes or until browned and tender, stirring frequently. Transfer to large bowl to cool slightly.

3 Place beans in small microwavable bowl; microwave on HIGH 1 minute or until heated through. Add beans, cilantro and chipotle pepper to corn; mix well. Pour lime juice mixture over corn mixture; stir gently to coat.

NOTE

Chipotle peppers in adobo sauce are available canned in the Mexican food section of most supermarkets. Since only a small amount is needed for this dish, spoon leftovers into a covered food storage container and refrigerate or freeze.

JALAPEÑO COLE SLAW

6 cups shredded cabbage or coleslaw mix

2 medium fresh tomatoes, seeded and chopped

6 green onions, coarsely chopped

2 jalapeño peppers, finely chopped

¼ cup cider vinegar

3 tablespoons honey

1 teaspoon salt

1 Combine cabbage, tomatoes, green onions, jalapeños, vinegar, honey and salt in large serving bowl; mix well. Cover; chill at least 2 hours before serving.

2 Stir well immediately before serving.

TIP

For a milder coleslaw, discard the seeds and veins when chopping the jalapeños, as this is where much of the heat of the pepper is stored.

MEXICAN-STYLE RICE AND CHEESE

1 can (about 15 ounces) Mexican-style beans

1 can (about 14 ounces) diced tomatoes with green chiles

2 cups (8 ounces) shredded Monterey Jack or Colby cheese, divided

1½ cups uncooked converted long grain rice

1 large onion, finely chopped

½ (8-ounce) package cream cheese

3 cloves garlic, minced

SLOW COOKER DIRECTIONS

1 Coat inside of slow cooker with nonstick cooking spray. Combine beans, tomatoes with chiles, 1 cup Monterey Jack cheese, rice, onion, cream cheese and garlic in slow cooker; mix well.

2 Cover; cook on LOW 6 to 8 hours. Sprinkle with remaining 1 cup Monterey Jack cheese just before serving.

CONFETTI BLACK BEANS

1 cup dried black beans

3 cups water

1 can (about 14 ounces) chicken broth

1 bay leaf

1½ teaspoons olive oil

1 medium onion, chopped

¼ cup chopped red bell pepper

¼ cup chopped yellow bell pepper

2 cloves garlic, minced

1 jalapeño pepper, finely chopped

1 large tomato, seeded and chopped

½ teaspoon salt

⅛ teaspoon black pepper

Hot pepper sauce (optional)

1 Sort and rinse beans; cover with water. Soak 8 hours or overnight. Drain.

2 Combine beans and broth in large saucepan; bring to a boil over high heat. Add bay leaf. Reduce heat to low. Cover; simmer 1½ hours or until beans are tender.

3 Heat oil in large nonstick skillet over medium heat. Add onion, bell peppers, garlic and jalapeño pepper; cook and stir 8 to 10 minutes or until onion is translucent. Add tomato, salt and black pepper; cook 5 minutes.

4 Add onion mixture to beans; cook 15 to 20 minutes.

5 Remove and discard bay leaf. Serve with hot pepper sauce, if desired.

MEXICAN CORN BREAD PUDDING

1 can (14¾ ounces) cream-style corn

2 eggs

1 can (4 ounces) diced mild green chiles

2 tablespoons vegetable oil

¾ cup yellow cornmeal

2 tablespoons sugar

2 teaspoons baking powder

¾ teaspoon salt

½ cup (2 ounces) shredded Cheddar cheese

SLOW COOKER DIRECTIONS

Coat 2-quart slow cooker with nonstick cooking spray. Combine corn, eggs, chiles, oil, cornmeal, sugar, baking powder and salt in medium bowl; stir well to blend. Pour into slow cooker. Cover; cook on LOW 2 to 2½ hours or until center is set. Sprinkle cheese over top. Cover; let stand 5 minutes or until cheese is melted.

PICANTE PINTOS AND RICE

- 2 cups dried pinto beans, rinsed and sorted
- 2 cups water
- 1 can (about 14 ounces) stewed tomatoes
- 1 cup coarsely chopped onion
- ¾ cup coarsely chopped green bell pepper
- ¼ cup sliced celery
- 4 cloves garlic, minced
- ½ small jalapeño pepper, seeded and chopped
- 2 teaspoons dried oregano
- 2 teaspoons chili powder
- ½ teaspoon ground red pepper
- 2 cups chopped kale
- 3 cups hot cooked brown rice

1 Place beans in large saucepan; add water to cover beans by 2 inches. Bring to a boil over high heat; boil 2 minutes. Remove from heat; let stand, covered, 1 hour. Drain beans; discard water. Return beans to saucepan.

2 Add 2 cups water, tomatoes, onion, bell pepper, celery, garlic, jalapeño pepper, oregano, chili powder and red pepper to saucepan; bring to a boil over high heat. Reduce heat to low. Simmer, covered, about 1½ hours or until beans are tender, stirring occasionally.

3 Gently stir kale into bean mixture. Simmer, uncovered, 30 minutes. (Beans will be very tender.) Serve over rice.

CHILE AND LIME QUINOA

½ cup uncooked quinoa

1 cup water

1 small jalapeño pepper, minced

2 tablespoons finely chopped green onion

2 tablespoons olive oil

1 tablespoon fresh lime juice

¼ teaspoon salt

¼ teaspoon ground cumin

¼ teaspoon chili powder

⅛ teaspoon black pepper

1 Place quinoa in fine-mesh strainer; rinse well under cold running water.

2 Bring 1 cup water and quinoa in small saucepan to a boil over high heat. Reduce heat to low. Cover; simmer 12 to 15 minutes or until quinoa is tender and water is absorbed. Cover; let stand 5 minutes.

3 Stir jalapeño pepper, green onion, oil, lime juice, salt, cumin, chili powder and black pepper into quinoa. Fluff mixture with fork. Serve warm or at room temperature.

NOTE

Quinoa is a grain with a flavor similar to couscous and cooks up quicker than rice. Look for it in the rice and dried beans section or in the natural foods aisle of your supermarket.

DESSERTS & DRINKS

CLASSIC FLAN

1½ **cups sugar, divided**
1 **tablespoon water**
¼ **teaspoon ground cinnamon**
3 **cups whole milk**
3 **eggs**
3 **egg yolks**
1 **teaspoon vanilla**

1 Preheat oven to 300°F.

2 Combine 1 cup sugar, water and cinnamon in medium saucepan; cook over medium-high heat without stirring 10 minutes or until sugar is melted and mixture is deep golden amber in color. Pour into six 6-ounce ramekins, swirling to coat bottoms. Place ramekins in 13×9-inch baking pan.

3 Heat milk in separate medium saucepan over medium heat until bubbles begin to form around edge of pan.

4 Meanwhile, whisk eggs, egg yolks, vanilla and remaining ½ cup sugar in medium bowl until well blended. Whisk in ½ cup hot milk in thin, steady stream. Gradually whisk in remaining milk. Divide milk mixture evenly among ramekins. Carefully add hot water to baking pan until water comes halfway up sides of ramekins. Cover ramekins with waxed paper or parchment paper.

5 Bake 1 hour 15 minutes or until custard is firm and knife inserted into custard comes out clean. Remove ramekins from baking pan to wire rack; cool completely. Cover and refrigerate until cold. Run small knife around edges of ramekins; invert flan onto serving plates.

CLASSIC MARGARITA

Lime wedges
Coarse salt
Ice
4 ounces tequila
2 ounces triple sec
2 ounces lime or lemon juice
Additional lime wedges

1 Rub rim of margarita glasses with lime wedges; dip in salt.

2 Fill cocktail shaker with ice; add tequila, triple sec and lime juice. Shake until blended; strain into glasses. Garnish with additional lime wedges.

FROZEN MARGARITA

Rub rim of margarita glasses with lime wedges; dip in salt. Combine tequila, triple sec, lime juice and 2 cups ice in blender; blend until smooth. Pour into prepared glasses; garnish with lime wedges. Makes 2 servings.

STRAWBERRY MARGARITA

Rub rim of margarita glasses with lime wedges; dip in salt, if desired. Fill glasses with ice. Combine tequila, triple sec, lime juice, 1 cup strawberries in blender; blend until smooth. Pour into prepared glasses; garnish with lime wedges and/or fresh mint sprigs. Makes 2 servings.

MEXICAN SUGAR COOKIES

2½ cups shortening
2 cups sugar, divided
1 teaspoon ground anise seeds
2 eggs
¼ cup orange juice
6 cups all-purpose flour
1 tablespoon baking powder
½ teaspoon cream of tartar
½ teaspoon salt
3 tablespoons ground cinnamon

1 Beat shortening, 1 cup sugar and anise with electric mixer at medium speed until creamy. Add eggs, one at a time, beating after each addition. Add orange juice; beat until light and fluffy.

2 Combine flour, baking powder, cream of tartar and salt in separate large bowl. Gradually beat into shortening mixture to form dough.

3 Knead dough on lightly floured surface. Form dough into two discs; wrap in plastic wrap. Refrigerate 30 minutes.

4 Preheat oven to 350°F. Line cookie sheets with parchment paper.

5 Working with one disc at a time, roll out dough on lightly floured surface to ½-inch thickness. Cut with cookie cutters. Gently press dough trimmings together; reroll and cut out more cookies. Place on prepared cookie sheets.

6 Bake 5 to 8 minutes or until light brown. Remove from oven. Combine remaining 1 cup sugar and cinnamon in small bowl. Sprinkle warm cookies with cinnamon-sugar mixture. Cool completely on wire racks.

SPANISH CHURROS
WITH HOT FUDGE SAUCE

CHURROS

- 1 cup water
- ¼ cup (½ stick) butter
- 6 tablespoons sugar, divided
- ¼ teaspoon salt
- 1 cup all-purpose flour
- 2 eggs
  Vegetable oil for frying
- 1 teaspoon ground cinnamon

HOT FUDGE SAUCE

- 2 cups whipping cream
- ½ cup light corn syrup
- ¾ cup packed dark brown sugar
- ⅓ cup cocoa powder
- 1 teaspoon kosher salt
- 8 ounces bittersweet chocolate, chopped
- ¼ cup (½ stick) tablespoons cold unsalted butter

1 For churros, place water, ¼ cup butter, 2 tablespoons sugar and ¼ teaspoon salt in medium saucepan; bring to a boil over high heat. Remove from heat; add flour. Beat with spoon until dough forms ball and releases from side of pan. Vigorously beat in eggs, one at a time, until mixture is smooth. Spoon dough into pastry bag fitted with large star tip. Pipe 3×1-inch strips onto waxed paper-lined baking sheet. Freeze 20 minutes.

2 Pour oil into large skillet to ¾-inch depth. Heat oil to 375°F. Transfer frozen dough, 4 to 5 churros at a time, to hot oil with large spatula. Fry 3 to 4 minutes or until deep golden brown, turning once. Remove with slotted spoon to paper towels; drain.

3 Combine remaining 4 tablespoons sugar with cinnamon in paper bag. Add warm churros, one at a time. Close bag and shake until churros are coated with cinnamon-sugar mixture. Remove to wire rack; cool completely. Store tightly covered at room temperature or freeze up to 3 months.

4 For hot fudge sauce, combine cream, corn syrup and brown sugar in large saucepan. Heat over medium-high heat until mixture boils. Cook 2 minutes, stirring occasionally. Reduce heat to low. Whisk in cocoa, 1 teaspoon kosher salt and chocolate 1 minute or until chocolate is melted and mixture is smooth. Turn off heat; whisk in ¼ cup butter.

5 Cool to room temperature, whisking occasionally. Pour evenly into jars; seal. Keep refrigerated up to 2 weeks. Warm before serving to make pourable but still thick.

HORCHATA

MAKES 3 SERVINGS ▶

16 ounces KOZY SHACK® No
    Sugar Added Rice Pudding
5 ounces fat-free milk
1 tablespoon vanilla extract
1 tablespoon cinnamon
   Ice cubes, as desired

1 In a blender, mix all ingredients.

2 Serve in glasses over ice, as desired.

SALSA SIPPER

MAKES 1 SERVING

1 can (5.5 ounces) V8® 100%
    Vegetable Juice **or** Spicy
    Hot V8® Vegetable Juice
1½ ounces vodka
1 teaspoon lemon juice
   Dash Worcestershire sauce
   Dash hot pepper sauce
   Celery stalk for garnish

Stir the vegetable juice, vodka, lemon juice, Worcestershire and hot pepper sauce in a small pitcher. Serve over ice. Garnish with a celery stalk.

MEXICAN CHOCOLATE MACAROONS

8 ounces semisweet chocolate, divided
1¾ cups plus ⅓ cup whole almonds, divided
¾ cup sugar
½ teaspoon salt
2 egg whites
1 teaspoon ground cinnamon
1 teaspoon vanilla

1 Preheat oven to 400°F. Grease cookie sheets.

2 Place 5 ounces of chocolate in food processor; process until coarsely chopped. Add 1¾ cups almonds, sugar and salt; process using on/off pulses until mixture is finely ground. Add egg whites, cinnamon and vanilla; process just until mixture forms moist dough.

3 Shape dough into 1-inch balls. (Dough will be sticky.) Place 2 inches apart on prepared cookie sheets. Press 1 whole almond into center of each dough ball.

4 Bake 8 to 10 minutes or just until set. Cool on cookie sheets 2 minutes. Remove to wire racks; cool completely.

5 Melt remaining 3 ounces of chocolate. Place in small resealable food storage bag. Cut off small corner of bag. Drizzle chocolate over cookies. Let stand until set.

MEXICAN COFFEE
WITH CHOCOLATE AND CINNAMON

6 cups water
½ cup ground dark roast coffee
2 cinnamon sticks
1 cup half-and-half
⅓ cup chocolate syrup
¼ cup packed dark brown sugar
1½ teaspoons vanilla, divided
1 cup whipping cream
¼ cup powdered sugar
Ground cinnamon

1 Place water in drip coffee maker. Place coffee and cinnamon sticks in filter basket of coffee maker. Combine half-and-half, chocolate syrup, brown sugar and 1 teaspoon vanilla in coffee pot. Place coffee pot with cream mixture in coffee maker. Brew coffee; coffee will drip into chocolate cream mixture.

2 Meanwhile, beat cream in medium bowl with electric mixer at high speed until soft peaks form. Add powdered sugar and remaining ½ teaspoon vanilla; beat until stiff peaks form. Pour coffee into individual coffee cups; top with dollop of whipped cream. Sprinkle with ground cinnamon.

TRES LECHES CAKE

1 package (about 15 ounces) white cake mix, plus ingredients to prepare mix

1 can (14 ounces) sweetened condensed milk

1 cup milk

1 cup whipping cream

1 container (8 ounces) frozen whipped topping, thawed

Fresh fruit (optional)

1 Preheat oven to 350°F. Spray 13×9-inch baking pan with nonstick cooking spray.

2 Prepare cake mix according to package directions. Pour batter into prepared pan. Bake 30 minutes or until toothpick inserted into center comes out clean. Cool in pan 5 minutes.

3 Meanwhile, combine sweetened condensed milk, milk and cream in 4-cup measure. Poke holes into cake with toothpick. Slowly pour milk mixture evenly over top. Let stand 10 to 15 minutes to absorb liquid. Cover; refrigerate at least 1 hour.

4 Spread whipped topping over cake. Garnish with fruit. Cover; refrigerate until serving.

COCOA FLAN

1 cup sugar

1 can (5 ounces) evaporated whole milk*

Water

¼ cup HERSHEY'S® Cocoa

1 can (14 ounces) sweetened condensed milk

4 eggs

2 teaspoons vanilla extract

¼ teaspoon salt

1¼ cups whole milk may be substituted for the reconstituted evaporated milk.

1 Heat oven to 325°F. Heat sugar in heavy medium skillet or saucepan over medium-low heat, stirring occasionally, until melted and golden brown. Pour into bottom of 1½-quart baking dish.

2 Pour evaporated milk into 2-cup glass measuring cup; add water to make 1¼ cups. Place cocoa in medium bowl; add enough of the reconstituted milk to form a paste and then gradually blend in the remaining milk.

3 Place chocolate milk mixture, sweetened condensed milk, eggs, vanilla and salt in blender container. Cover; blend until smooth and well blended. Gradually pour over sugar mixture in baking dish. Cover top of baking dish with foil to keep it from browning.

4 Set dish in a larger baking pan. Fill the larger pan with water until it reaches halfway up sides of dish. Bake 1½ to 2 hours or until knife comes out almost clean when inserted halfway into center of custard. (Do not pierce bottom.) Remove from water to wire rack. Cool 2 hours. Cover; refrigerate overnight or until thoroughly chilled (about 8 hours).

5 To serve, run a knife or rubber scraper along the outside of the flan. Place serving plate over baking dish; invert onto serving plate. Let stand several minutes for the flan to release and the topping to drip down; remove baking dish. Garnish as desired.

HONEY SOPAIPILLAS

¼ cup plus 2 teaspoons sugar, divided
½ teaspoon ground cinnamon
2 cups all-purpose flour
½ teaspoon salt
2 teaspoons baking powder
2 tablespoons shortening
¾ cup warm water
  Vegetable oil for deep-frying
  Honey

1 Combine ¼ cup sugar and cinnamon in small bowl; set aside. Combine remaining 2 teaspoons sugar, flour, salt and baking powder in large bowl. Cut in shortening with pastry blender or two knives until mixture resembles fine crumbs. Gradually add water; stir with fork until mixture forms dough. Turn out onto lightly floured surface; knead 2 minutes or until smooth. Shape into a ball; cover with bowl and let rest 30 minutes.

2 Divide dough into four equal portions; shape each into a ball. Flatten each ball into 8-inch circle ⅛ inch thick. Cut each round into four wedges.

3 Pour oil into electric skillet or deep heavy skillet to depth of 1½ inches. Heat to 360°F. Cook dough, two pieces at a time, 2 minutes or until puffed and golden brown, turning once during cooking. Remove from oil with slotted spoon; drain on paper towels. Sprinkle with cinnamon-sugar mixture. Repeat with remaining sopaipillas. Serve warm with honey.

MEXICAN MACARONS

COOKIES

- 1 cup powdered sugar
- ½ cup almond flour
- 3 tablespoons unsweetened cocoa powder
- ½ teaspoon ground cinnamon
- 2 egg whites, at room temperature
- ¼ cup granulated sugar

FILLING

- 3½ ounces bittersweet chocolate, finely chopped
- ½ cup whipping cream
- 2 tablespoons butter
- ¼ teaspoon ground cinnamon
- ¼ teaspoon ground red pepper

1 For cookies, line two cookie sheets with parchment paper. Combine powdered sugar, almond flour, cocoa and ½ teaspoon cinnamon in food processor. Pulse into fine powder, scraping bowl occasionally. Sift mixture into medium bowl.

2 Beat egg whites in large bowl with electric mixer at high speed about 1 minute or until foamy. Gradually add granulated sugar, beating at high speed 2 to 3 minutes or until mixture forms stiff, shiny peaks, scraping bowl occasionally.

3 Add half of flour mixture to egg whites. Stir with spatula to combine (about 12 strokes). Repeat with remaining flour mixture. Mix about 15 strokes more by pressing against side of bowl and scooping from bottom until batter is smooth and shiny. Check consistency by dropping spoonful of batter onto plate. It should have a peak which quickly relaxes back into batter. (Do not overmix or undermix.)

4 Attach ½-inch plain tip to piping bag. Scoop batter into bag. Pipe 1-inch circles about 2 inches apart onto prepared cookie sheets. Rap cookie sheets on flat surface to remove air bubbles and set aside. Let macarons rest, uncovered, until tops harden slightly; this takes from 15 minutes on dry days to 1 hour in more humid conditions. Gently touch top of macaron to check. When batter does not stick, macarons are ready to bake.

5 Preheat oven to 350°F. Place rack in center of oven. Bake 13 to 15 minutes, rotating cookie sheets halfway through baking time. Cool completely on cookie sheets. When cooling, if cookies appear to

be sticking to parchment, lift parchment edges and spray pan underneath lightly with water. Steam will help release cookies.

6 For filling, place chocolate in medium bowl. Heat cream and butter to a simmer in small saucepan over medium-high heat. Remove from heat; stir in ¼ teaspoon cinnamon and red pepper. Pour over chocolate; let stand 3 minutes. Stir until smooth. Let stand until thickened.

7 Match same size cookies; pipe or spread filling on flat side of one cookie and top with another.

CINNAMON DESSERT TACOS
WITH FRUIT SALSA

1 cup sliced fresh strawberries
1 cup cubed fresh pineapple
1 cup cubed peeled kiwi
½ teaspoon minced jalapeño
    pepper
4 tablespoons sugar, divided
1 tablespoon ground cinnamon
6 (8-inch) flour tortillas

1 Combine strawberries, pineapple, kiwi, jalapeño and 1 tablespoon sugar in large bowl; stir to blend. Set aside. Combine 3 tablespoons sugar and cinnamon in small bowl; set aside.

2 Spray tortilla lightly on both sides with nonstick cooking spray. Heat over medium heat in nonstick skillet until slightly puffed and golden brown. Remove from heat; immediately dust both sides with cinnamon-sugar mixture. Shake excess cinnamon-sugar back into bowl. Repeat until all tortillas are warmed.

3 Fill tortillas with fruit mixture and fold in half. Serve immediately.

ICED MEXICAN COFFEE

½ cup regular or decaffeinated
   ground dark roast coffee

4 cups water

1 tablespoon sugar

⅔ cup half-and-half or milk

¼ cup chocolate syrup

1 teaspoon vanilla

½ teaspoon cinnamon extract*
   Ice cubes

*Or, omit cinnamon extract and
break two 3-inch-long cinnamon
sticks into several pieces. Place
cinnamon pieces in filter basket of
coffee maker with ground coffee.
Continue as directed.*

1 Place ground coffee in filter basket of coffee maker. Add water to coffee maker and brew according to manufacturer's directions. Pour coffee into 4-cup heatproof measuring cup or small pitcher. Add sugar; stir until dissolved. Cover; cool to room temperature.

2 Combine half-and-half, chocolate syrup, vanilla and cinnamon extract in small bowl; blend well. Stir into cooled coffee. Serve immediately in ice-filled glasses.

"MEXICAN" BROWNIES

1 package (about 19 ounces) brownie mix, plus ingredients to prepare mix

2 teaspoons ground cinnamon

1 package (8 ounces) cream cheese, softened

½ cup dulce de leche (see Note)

2 tablespoons powdered sugar

1 Prepare and bake brownies according to package directions, stirring cinnamon into batter. Cool completely in pan on wire rack.

2 Beat cream cheese in medium bowl with electric mixer at medium speed until smooth. Add dulce de leche and powdered sugar; beat until well blended and creamy.

3 Spread frosting over brownies. Serve immediately or refrigerate overnight for richer flavor.

NOTE

Dulce de leche is caramelized condensed milk widely used in Mexican desserts. It is sold in cans in most large supermarkets. You can prepare your our own dulce de leche by heating 1 cup whole milk and ½ cup granulated sugar just to a boil; reduce heat to medium-low and cook 30 minutes or until caramel in color, stirring occasionally. Remove from heat; cool completely. Stir in ¼ teaspoon vanilla. If using homemade dulce de leche, omit the powdered sugar from the recipe.

MEXICAN WEDDING COOKIES

1 cup pecan pieces or halves

1 cup (2 sticks) butter, softened

2 cups powdered sugar, divided

2 cups all-purpose flour

2 teaspoons vanilla

⅛ teaspoon salt

1 Place pecans in food processor or blender; process using on/off pulses until pecans are ground but not pasty.

2 Beat butter and ½ cup powdered sugar in large bowl with electric mixer at medium speed until light and fluffy. Gradually add 1 cup flour, vanilla and salt at low speed, beating until well blended. Stir in remaining 1 cup flour and ground nuts. Shape dough into a ball; wrap in plastic wrap. Refrigerate 1 hour or until firm.

3 Preheat oven to 350°F. Shape dough into 1-inch balls. Place 1 inch apart on ungreased cookie sheets.

4 Bake 12 to 15 minutes or until golden brown. Cool on cookie sheets 2 minutes.

5 Meanwhile, place 1 cup powdered sugar in 13×9-inch baking dish. Transfer hot cookies to powdered sugar. Roll cookies in powdered sugar, coating well. Let cookies cool in sugar in dish.

6 Sift remaining ½ cup powdered sugar over cookies just before serving. Store tightly covered at room temperature or freeze up to 1 month.

Acknowledgments

The publisher would like to thank the companies listed below for the use of their recipes and photographs in this publication.

Campbell Soup Company

Heinz North America

The Hershey Company

Kozy Shack Enterprises, Inc.

McCormick®

Riviana Foods Inc.

Unilever

METRIC CONVERSION CHART

VOLUME MEASUREMENTS (dry)

$1/8$ teaspoon = 0.5 mL
$1/4$ teaspoon = 1 mL
$1/2$ teaspoon = 2 mL
$3/4$ teaspoon = 4 mL
1 teaspoon = 5 mL
1 tablespoon = 15 mL
2 tablespoons = 30 mL
$1/4$ cup = 60 mL
$1/3$ cup = 75 mL
$1/2$ cup = 125 mL
$2/3$ cup = 150 mL
$3/4$ cup = 175 mL
1 cup = 250 mL
2 cups = 1 pint = 500 mL
3 cups = 750 mL
4 cups = 1 quart = 1 L

VOLUME MEASUREMENTS (fluid)

1 fluid ounce (2 tablespoons) = 30 mL
4 fluid ounces ($1/2$ cup) = 125 mL
8 fluid ounces (1 cup) = 250 mL
12 fluid ounces ($1 1/2$ cups) = 375 mL
16 fluid ounces (2 cups) = 500 mL

WEIGHTS (mass)

$1/2$ ounce = 15 g
1 ounce = 30 g
3 ounces = 90 g
4 ounces = 120 g
8 ounces = 225 g
10 ounces = 285 g
12 ounces = 360 g
16 ounces = 1 pound = 450 g

DIMENSIONS

$1/16$ inch = 2 mm
$1/8$ inch = 3 mm
$1/4$ inch = 6 mm
$1/2$ inch = 1.5 cm
$3/4$ inch = 2 cm
1 inch = 2.5 cm

OVEN TEMPERATURES

250°F = 120°C
275°F = 140°C
300°F = 150°C
325°F = 160°C
350°F = 180°C
375°F = 190°C
400°F = 200°C
425°F = 220°C
450°F = 230°C

BAKING PAN SIZES

Utensil	Size in Inches/Quarts	Metric Volume	Size in Centimeters
Baking or Cake Pan (square or rectangular)	$8 \times 8 \times 2$	2 L	$20 \times 20 \times 5$
	$9 \times 9 \times 2$	2.5 L	$23 \times 23 \times 5$
	$12 \times 8 \times 2$	3 L	$30 \times 20 \times 5$
	$13 \times 9 \times 2$	3.5 L	$33 \times 23 \times 5$
Loaf Pan	$8 \times 4 \times 3$	1.5 L	$20 \times 10 \times 7$
	$9 \times 5 \times 3$	2 L	$23 \times 13 \times 7$
Round Layer Cake Pan	$8 \times 1 1/2$	1.2 L	20×4
	$9 \times 1 1/2$	1.5 L	23×4
Pie Plate	$8 \times 1 1/4$	750 mL	20×3
	$9 \times 1 1/4$	1 L	23×3
Baking Dish or Casserole	1 quart	1 L	—
	$1 1/2$ quart	1.5 L	—
	2 quart	2 L	—